IN OTHER NEWS

REPORTERS ON REPORTING

To all the journalists who aspire to be truly great
and spark change while holding power accountable
and giving the voiceless an opportunity to speak

CONTENTS

Photo credit: courtesy of Mara Leveritt

Chapter 1

MARA LEVERITT

TWENTY-THREE YEARS HAVE PASSED SINCE the horrifying murders of three 8-year-old boys took place in West Memphis, Arkansas. To this day it is unclear who committed the unthinkable act, but thanks to Mara Leveritt's persistent coverage of the case, it is clearer who did *not* commit the crimes.

Damien Echols, Jason Baldwin, and Jessie Misskelley, Jr.—commonly known as the West Memphis Three—spent the better part of their young adult lives in prison. Convicted as teenagers, the three were locked away for 18 years. Some could argue they were lucky to get out that early, especially "Ringleader" Echols who, 18 years old at the time of his sentence, was put on Death Row for his alleged involvement in killing the three second graders.

The small-town crime quickly became a national media circus, and HBO even sent a crew down to the small Arkansas town to film a documentary. Between the reputations of the local politicians and West Memphis law enforcement, the pressure was mounting for the case to be solved—and quickly.

Satanism was ruled as a factor early on, and the three boys were arrested, mainly due to Echols' affiliation and fascination with witchcraft. There were several witnesses who testified against the young men in court, but years later many of those witnesses recanted their statements.

There was no DNA evidence that tied any of the suspects to the crime scene. There was, however, a confession from one of the boys, which was later deemed to be provoked by law enforcement;

many of the details of the alleged crime did not add up. Misskelley, the confessor, had a known mental disability, not to mention an alibi for the night of the murder that supposedly placed him at a wrestling practice with his classmates.

Today, looking back at the trials, it's easy to see how riddled with errors the case really was. But at the time, questioning the state's decision wasn't as popular a stance. "I was the only one writing about the case here and expressing concern about the quality of the convictions," Mara said.

Regardless of any media coverage, the boys were sentenced to life without parole. That's where the reporting could have easily ended, but that's when things really heated up for Mara. She continued to investigate the crimes for several years because she was not convinced the state had put the right people behind bars.

Keep in mind that she was essentially asking for the release of three "punk teenagers" who were allegedly involved in the brutal killings of three 8-year-old boys who went missing after school on May 5, 1993.

The day after their disappearance, those boys were found dead in a nearby creek close to Robin Hood Hills. They were naked, hog-tied, and they appeared to have been sexually mutilated.

Mara has dedicated the past 20-plus years to figuring out who could be capable of such a heinous crime. She wasn't the first person to question the boys' innocence, but she'll definitely go down in history for her thorough reporting of the case. Bob Lancaster of the *Arkansas Times*, she said, was actually the first to write a column posing a contradictory view to what most media outlets were reporting.

When Mara read the local columnist's piece, she really stopped in her tracks, acknowledged its merit, and fiercely changed directions with her coverage. She just did not see enough valid evidence that made the boys murderers. In her opinion the facts—or lack thereof—weren't convincing enough.

Within weeks of Damien's sentencing, Mara reached out to him for an interview. He agreed, and she wrote a cover story about him for the *Arkansas Times,* "Witch on Death Row."

Damien was the first person Mara wrote to, requesting an interview. "I did not have contact with any of the accused before their convictions," she explained.

It wasn't until 1998 that Mara reached out to Jason. "We established a correspondence then that continues to this day," she said. "I also visited Jessie in 1998, and we have had sporadic visits and letters ever since. I think all of this was possible because, first, my paper, and thereafter I personally, had written with some skepticism about their trials—something no other media were doing."

Mara maintained a relationship with the three accused and was so intrigued by them that she decided to write a book about the story. "When I started to write *Devil's Knot,* my friends said, 'Mara, they did it.' And I said, 'Well, that may be, and if that's true I'm gonna find out,'" she said in her interview for the Peter Jackson-backed documentary about the murders, *West of Memphis.*

Years earlier Mara also appeared in a separate documentary, the *Paradise Lost* trilogy, produced by HBO. There she shared her knowledge of the case and her doubts behind the convictions. She has separately been interviewed as an expert source by CBS for *This Morning* and the crime investigation series *48 Hours.*

Her connection to the case has become, no doubt, deep-rooted. And her watchdog reporting all started with her simple observations from the trials that subsequently turned into interviews and later into many follow-ups with the three young men who were convicted.

But this wasn't the first time Mara sank her teeth into a case like this, nor was it the first time she turned her reporting into a book. Prior to her tale about Damien, Jason, and Jessie, she had a pair of other teenage boys who demanded her attention.

In 1999 her book, *The Boys on the Tracks: Death, Denial and a Mother's Crusade to Bring Her Son's Killer to Justice,* was published by St. Martin's Press. Again Mara had found herself drawn to bringing justice to a complicated and flawed case.

This time two Arkansas teenagers were run over by a train, and the state medical examiner ruled they had died in a "marijuana-induced stupor." But later one of the children's parents ordered an independent autopsy, which concluded it was no accident but, in fact, murder.

In Mara's blog she described the book to be "about a corrupt prosecutor who manipulated his position to derail the investigation ... The mother of one of the murdered boys trusted him—as did everyone—but he betrayed them all."

That mother, Linda Ives, "assembled evidence that the boys had stumbled upon a diffuse conspiracy involving CIA-backed air suppliers to the Contras who ran an enormous cocaine-trafficking operation from a remote airport," Mara's synopsis of the book reads.

Mara took a journey with the mother to document how this case was flawed due to the work of local agencies, state police, and the FBI. "I think when things go right, that's wonderful," Mara said. "But there are things that go badly wrong, and those stories need to be told."

The book did well and received myriad awards and praise, including the review from *Publishers Weekly* that described the book as "a true-crime thriller by an established investigative journalist ... The action grips readers from the beginning."

So when Mara turned around to pen *Devil's Knot: The True Story of the West Memphis Three*, she initially didn't expect it to be so difficult to land the book deal. She thought she had proven herself as an author, but unfortunately, she found publishing contracts don't always work that way.

After shopping around the idea with her agent at the time, the book was finally published in 2002 by Atria Books, a subsidiary of Simon & Schuster Inc. As with her first book, *Devil's Knot* scored another Booker Worthen Literary Prize for Mara, who was selected as an honoree among Arkansas' finest authors.

The story became a cult phenomenon, albeit a controversial one, and was eventually turned into a film starring Reese Witherspoon and Colin Firth in 2013.

To this day, *Devil's Knot* is the most comprehensive account of the murders of Stevie Branch, Michael Moore, and Christopher Byers, according to reviewers.

One review of *Devil's Knot* said, "The abuses of the criminal justice system shown here are so blatant—and so profoundly tragic—that they would be hard to believe were it not for the depth and evenhandedness of Leveritt's reporting." That testimonial came from Sister Helen Prejean, author of the best-seller *Dead Man Walking: The Eyewitness Account of the Death Penalty that Sparked a National Debate.*

To tell the story, Mara scoured through court transcripts and police logs, as well as videos of witness interviews and those of the suspects. She also spent months interviewing key people in the case, including the West Memphis Three and the victims' families, in addition to law enforcement.

"Mara is a powerhouse," said Jason Baldwin through a private message on Facebook. That was in late 2014, around the time the two were co-authoring a book together. He also called her "a true champion for the cause of justice" to his followers on Facebook:

> Mara Leveritt refuses to give in to injustice. She continues the fight in Arkansas for the full and complete exoneration of Damien Echols, Jessie Lloyd Misskelley, Jr., and myself. She doesn't stop there. She calls for the powers that be in the state of Arkansas to declare the case of the murders of Michael Moore, Steve Branch and Christopher Byers unsolved. When she succeeds in her efforts, the perpetrator(s) will then know that his/her/their time is up for the Great State of Arkansas will then be utilizing all the powers it has at its disposal to pursue. Thank you Mara for never giving up.

Mara is close with her sources now, but in the beginning she wasn't connected at all. As with any coverage of a highly sensitive situation, it was a challenge to get information. She had to know what she was after and settle for nothing less. Reaching out to the West Memphis Three began similarly to all of the other cases Mara has reported on: with a letter to the convicted person or people.

Mara considers herself lucky to have been granted access to the West Memphis Three because not all inmates are open to speaking with the media. "I think reporters should introduce themselves as thoroughly as possible when seeking an interview, and realize that, even then, there are many reasons why inmates may not respond," she said. "Some are too low-functioning, mentally disorganized, suspicious, or intimidated to write to a member of the media. Some, realistically or not, fear retaliation from guards if they speak to media. Others, especially those who have appeals pending, will refuse on advice of attorneys."

In terms of the logistics in Arkansas, Mara noted, letters to inmates must include the person's inmate number assigned by the Department of Correction, which is available online for all prisoners.

"I write to the inmate first to introduce myself and say that I will be seeking an interview. The official request must be sent to the PIO (Public Information Officer) for the Department of Correction. If the inmate is not in some kind of punitive detention and can meet with media, the PIO will relay the request to the inmate. If the inmate agrees, the PIO contacts the reporter to establish a time."

Mara suggests that journalists clarify exactly what can and cannot be brought to the interview. "Cell phones (for photography) are universally banned. But, depending on the place and circumstances, I have been allowed to bring in a video camera, an audio recorder, and even an iPad for still photos," she said.

Before going to a prison, reporters should know prison policies regarding media, she said. "Here (in Arkansas), media visits are supposed to be confidential. However, on many occasions I have had guards and even the PIO settle into a chair within hearing distance. A polite request for privacy, with reference to policy, has always resulted in the chair being moved."

Her expertise within the courtroom has helped her establish experience with the topics she addresses throughout her books—three have been written so far—which all have the running theme of prosecutors and politics.

Mara's latest book was released in late 2014. After *Devil's Knot* gained such recognition, she decided to write a trilogy. *Dark Spell* was co-written with one of the West Memphis Three, Jason Baldwin. The story tells about Baldwin's experiences in prison. He entered the court system at the young age of 16 and left when he was 34 years old. He saw a lot within the prisons where he resided, and Mara wanted to capture what he experienced so readers could learn about the injustices happening right inside prison walls.

Dark Spell has not taken off quite like *Devil's Knot* did; nonetheless, it has attracted a substantial audience. As for Mara's decision to focus the book on Jason's experience specifically, she had her reasons. "Damien was already writing. Jason was pretty much off the radar," she said. "He didn't have quite the charismatic personality that Damien had; he didn't have a death sentence. [He and Jessie] didn't have [investigators] working on their behalf. Jason's story was more typical of most people serving life sentences."

Mara intends to write a third installment for the series, but she hasn't quite decided what it will be about. "It has to be something different than what has been written in the media," she said. "It will have to tell something with a new slant that is worthwhile."

Today, as she plugs away at a book about CIA drug smuggler Barry Seal, Mara works as the contributing editor for the *Arkansas Times*. She pitches stories as she sees fit and also spends time advocating for civil rights, specifically within the state of Arkansas. Mara calls herself an "extreme journalist" because of it. "I say 'extreme journalism' with a certain tongue-in-cheek because it sounds cool, and it's the closest I'll ever come to extreme sports," she joked. "And of course it's not for everyone. But I do believe that most reporters run into stories they realize open to greater depths than can be plumbed in a few days, weeks, or even years. I've been fortunate to be able to dive into a few of those."

That in-depth coverage has been recognized by many. One of her latest achievements was in 2014 when she received the Porter Fund Literary Prize from the nonprofit organization that recognizes Arkansas writers and poets.

Aside from the journalism rewards and praise are the straight-forward results from her journalism.

In November 2011 Mara sued the Arkansas Supreme Court's Committee on Professional Conduct. Through her reporting, she discovered that public complaints against the prosecuting attorneys in Arkansas weren't allowed. If someone made a complaint about a prosecutor and then reported it, the Supreme Court's disciplinary office threatened the reporter with a charge of contempt of court and punishment by fine and jail.

Mara contended that this restraint violated the nation's First Amendment, and she reported on the prosecutors anyway. "I wrote letters to the office involved. I wrote articles. I blogged. And for years I got blown off. Finally, I filed a federal civil rights lawsuit against the Arkansas Supreme Court. That got the state's attention," Mara blogged on her website.

A year later, the state settled the lawsuit by agreeing to end the practice. "I'd say that was the proudest moment in my career," Mara said.

Mara's work has made an impact on many levels, so much so that sometimes she finds herself bombarded with requests from people urging her to investigate a criminal case on their behalf. "I wish I had the time to dedicate to all of them, but I usually encourage them to find a reporter in their area," she said. "I wish I could set up a school for investigative journalism to train reporters to know what to look for in these cases."

Mara does use her influence, though, where she can. She regularly gives lectures and shares news about interesting cases with

her followers on social media. Albeit a stretch from leading an institution solely dedicated to investigative reporting, it is a platform she uses to get the word out about certain "social injustices," as she described them.

She fights on for freedom of the wrongfully convicted, and because she believes everyone deserves the chance of a fair trial, she frequently writes about "cryptolaw." She coined the term to explain how plain language is often distorted by members of the legal system, to the detriment of public trust.

One thing, in Mara's opinion, that would help with transparency within the legal system is the implementation of video cameras inside courtrooms. "These are official functions. We should get to see them," Mara argued in a YouTube series created by the *Arkansas Times* in 2014.

Mara laid out her views of how she thinks all police interactions should be filmed, particularly those within a courtroom. Then, she said, those DVDs should be made available to the public for the cost of the DVD. This, she said, sidesteps the age-old predicament of reporters being entitled to obtain public records of court proceedings; but, she added, the cost of the transcriptions can quickly become astronomical.

"What would that do?" Mara asked in the video. "It would let people who have had cases that call for question, such as the West Memphis case, it would let those people—and they are all across the country, in every state—it would give them an opportunity to have what the West Memphis Three had, which is a video-recorded account of their trials.

"People could *see*. They would not have to spend thousands of dollars to get a transcript written and printed of a trial and then read through pages and pages and pages. They could sit down and watch it. *That's* what makes the West Memphis case different. That existed because HBO, Joe Berlinger, and Bruce Sinofsky came to Arkansas and filmed it. Everybody should have that opportunity."

As for her involvement with the West Memphis Three, she continues to advocate their innocence. "Twenty years later, I am still writing about this case because it isn't over yet," Mara wrote on her website.

Mara hasn't fought this battle alone though. Far from it. There were several requests to appeal the original verdict, multiple people worked on the case *pro bono*, celebrities like Johnny Depp and Eddie Vedder stepped in to raise awareness, and community activist groups were started solely to speak up about the West Memphis Three case.

Ultimately, the men were released from prison in 2011. But it came with a catch: the three were released in a rare scenario, under the Alford Plea, which allowed the men to leave prison based on time served but while admitting guilt in order to be set free. They also had to agree not to sue the state of Arkansas for the wrongful conviction.

Mara still holds out hope that the case will someday be solved, but she's thankful for the "WM3" supporters. She fondly recalled the very first phone call she received in 1996 from a man named Grove Pashley, whom she refers to as the "first of the WM3.org heroes."

"His passion and commitment were clear, and I was so excited. I felt that a spark from a fire in Arkansas had jumped across the country and ignited caring people. Suddenly, it seemed that there really was potential, through media that were just then emerging, to bring this case to justice. Of course I could not have imagined how convoluted the route would be, how long we would all be on it, or that, even when the men were freed, justice still would not have been served."

Mara recently donated all of her paperwork on the case to the Butler Center for Arkansas Studies, a department of the Central Arkansas Library System. She thinks it is an important part of the state's history and hopes it will serve a purpose for those who visit the library to research the trials.

The case has lived on for 20-plus years already, and Mara described a scene which convinced her that this is only the beginning. When the men accepted the Alford Plea back in 2011, they were sent to a room separate from the highly-covered press conference to sign off on paperwork. Meanwhile, for those people still sitting in the audience, "[the judge] made a lot of remarks, and he told us that 'I believe this case will be studied for at least 100 years.'"

West of Memphis is the most recent documentary about the case and was produced by Damien Echols and a team of filmmakers in 2012. In the final frame of the movie, these closing words appear on screen: "To everyone, everywhere, who ever sat down to write a letter, who stood up and said, 'This is not justice,' Please know you made a difference ... You made *all* the difference."

One might say that the men had a very particular type of person in mind when making such a statement filled with utter gratitude. Maybe even someone like Mara Leveritt.

Photo credit: Mel Melcon, *Los Angeles Times*

Chapter 2

CHRISTINA BELLANTONI

"HI, I'M CHRISTINA BELLANTONI. I want to move to D.C. and report on politics, and my investigation into a judge is going to get him thrown off the bench." This is just one example of Christina's enviable drive and go-getter attitude that has made her a success in the world of journalism.

When she made the above-mentioned phone call, she was working for the *Palo Alto Daily News*. She had been hired there to run her own tiny bureau in the sleepy Silicon Valley town of Los Gatos, now home to Netflix Inc. The job proved to be great training for a young journalist like Christina.

One of the first assignments given to her by her editor was to print the home addresses of each of the town's city council members. The editor acknowledged that it was a controversial thing to do. "They're going to hate you, but this is the spirit of what we do. This is public information," she remembers him telling her.

Christina said that she has carried that spirit with her during her entire career and that it was a great lesson in the importance of transparency and access to public information.

Prior to calling up the newsroom in Washington, D.C. and highlighting her own work on the case with the judge, she worked another high-profile case in Los Gatos. On November 26, 2002, a local teenager named Eric Quesada was killed in a drunk driving accident. Christina said in the small town it was pretty easy to find out the identity of the teenage driver who had caused the accident that killed Eric Quesada. The community had been talking, and the then 16-year-old Brian Ricks was sitting in jail.

At the time, her editor made the tough decision to print Ricks' name and photo right out of his school's yearbook. Now an experienced editor, Christina acknowledges things might have gone differently with her at the helm. "I'm not sure I would have made the same decision," she said. "But I learned a lot from the fact that he made the decision, and I had to put my name on the story."

Her first foray into journalism was a childhood newspaper in which she wrote about events in her neighborhood. She recalled that the lead item on the front page was, "Christina's Grandpa Gets New Car" because he had purchased a gold Subaru wagon. She sold the paper door to door for $2.

Christina said that she didn't grow up reading the newspaper but, instead, was obsessed with novels, especially those of Stephen King. She was raised by a single parent, and people used to question her mother as to why Christina was allowed to read King's books. Her mother's reply? "She *can*, and we have grown-up conversations about it. I think it's a good way for her to learn about the world."

King initially inspired Christina to be a novelist, and she was on the newspaper and yearbook staffs at Del Mar High School in San Jose.

While in high school, and then as a student at UC Berkeley, Christina worked as a receptionist at a car dealership. Her ability to expertly answer phones led to her initial job in journalism.

Her mother worked in the same office building as the *San Jose Business Journal*. She heard through the grapevine that they were hiring a receptionist and encouraged Christina to apply. So she walked in, and she was allowed to meet with the editor. Christina once again turned on her ambition and drive. "Here's why you should hire me!" she said. Except she wasn't talking about the receptionist job; initially, she tried to get him to hire her as a reporter.

Her ploy didn't work, because she had no reporting experience, but she did get that receptionist position. She didn't give up though. Essentially, she would pester the editor each day when he walked in, asking about extra work, and if there was anything newsworthy that she could help out with. One of her duties was to monitor the fax machine, and she would hold the editor's faxes back so that he was forced to ask her for them.

It was then that she self-admittedly got in his face, asking, "Do you have any projects for me?" She said she eventually wore him down and was allowed to help out on a research project.

One of the researchers eventually left the company, and Christina took over his job. She put in 35 hours a week while still a full-time student at Berkeley. After approximately eight months, they let her write a feature on a couple who had a local beekeeping business, thus leading to a position as a lifestyle reporter.

The *San Jose Business Journal's* publisher, Armon Mills, started a competitor in September 2000 called *Silicon Valley Biz Ink*. He reportedly poached people from the paper, and Christina went along for the ride. She worked as the researcher at *Biz Ink* until 2002, a year after she graduated from Berkeley.

She received her B.A. in Mass Communications but said she doesn't think it is necessary to study journalism in college. In fact, as an editor she often hires individuals with degrees in alternate subjects, like economics, language studies, history, or political science.

"That is far more relevant to what they'll be doing, because I want them to have a broader understanding of history and the humanities in a way I totally didn't get," she explained.

It was the 2000 presidential election that got her interested in political reporting. "I was very engaged in the first election I could vote in," she said. As she watched the reporters on TV waiting for Al Gore to speak to his supporters gathered at the War Memorial Auditorium in Nashville, she thought to herself, "I want to do that. That's what I want to be."

She recalled being so excited that she couldn't sleep, so instead she wrote her St. Louis-based boyfriend a letter, telling him how and why she was so excited.

Around this time someone in her life gave her some life-changing advice, "Look, if you want to do this, you should not be a business journalist." That led her to join the *Palo Alto Daily News*, where she got to cover California's 2003 recall election in which Governor Gray Davis was ousted and voters chose actor Arnold Schwarzenegger. Over 130 candidates were on the recall ballot that October, and Christina's coverage included information on the candidates from the San Jose area.

After that she covered the local city council, cops, and courts. As it turned out, Santa Clara County Superior Court Judge William Danser had been writing letters on official letterhead, asking the police to dismiss his son's parking tickets. "The judge had tried to use his position to pressure the police chief for $40 tickets," she explained.

She published the story in her paper and was cited by the *San Jose Mercury News*, her biggest competitor, the next day. The story led to a full-on investigation, and even though she didn't get to see the investigation all the way through, it was successful.

In 2004 Danser was convicted of a single felony and eight misdemeanors due to his penchant for helping friends on the San Jose Sharks hockey team and San Jose Earthquakes soccer team deal with their traffic ticket and DUI cases. At the time, Danser received a lifetime ban from serving as a judge and was disbarred. He eventually succeeded in getting his felony reduced to a misdemeanor.

At that point Christina was following the story from D.C., because she had been hired at *The Washington Times* after cold-calling the metro editor to tell him about uncovering Judge Danser's ethics scandal. She was entering entirely new territory, coming from the West Coast, and she was assigned to cover politics in Virginia, which at the time was deeply conservative.

Add to the mix that she thought *The Washington Times* was the most conservative newspaper in America, and Christina was in for a real challenge. "Because I came from California and went to Berkeley, they were basically convinced that I was a big liberal," she said.

Christina believes you can be a good journalist and still have personal political opinions. When Democrats she covered were skeptical of the newspaper, she reminded them she had to earn a good reputation by being fair to everyone. It worked, and covering Virginia politics led to great political connections at all levels of government.

After that she was able to fulfill her dream from a few years earlier by covering national politics. She described herself as the "squeaky wheel" in the newsroom who constantly told everyone what she wanted to do.

That ambition and confidence paid off in 2004 when she was sent to cover the Republican National Convention in New York City because another woman at the paper was unavailable. "I went, and I was the lowest person on the totem pole, and it was grueling, but it was so much fun," she described the experience. "They let me loose and I did a good job."

That coverage of the convention led to her next big assignment, a profile of then Presidential candidate John Kerry's wife, Teresa Heinz Kerry. She traveled with Heinz Kerry through four states for the article.

After covering the 2005 Virginia governor's race, Christina was promoted to report on Congress. As the 2008 Presidential election approached, the newsroom began to divvy up the assignments. The more experienced reporters got first dibs on Democratic candidates like Hillary Clinton, so Christina showed interest in then little-known candidate Barack Obama.

She remembers that her boss laughed and said to her, "Well, that's fine. You can cover him. He'll never win!" She acknowledged that the paper treated her quite well by giving her a credit card for expenses and allowing her to travel to battleground states like Iowa and New Hampshire.

In fact, "I was able to have this really great coverage of Democrats for a conservative paper," Christina said. That experience proved handy, because when Obama won the election, she was immediately tasked with the coveted White House beat.

She did that for a year, and while she loved the atmosphere, "the actual work is not that fun," she said. She's glad she never got jaded, though. "There's a lot of glamour in it, and I always tell people if you walk into that campus, and you see the White House there, and walk in the front door and you don't get a little pitter patter in your heart? You're in the wrong business!"

Her advice to young people is to remember that being human is always at the heart of the story. "Ultimately, this is a story about human beings," she said. "Real human interactions with the voters. Human interactions with how they feel about a candidate."

For Christina the hardest thing about covering politics was breaking through. She mentioned standing in a cornfield in Iowa with 300 other reporters, covering Hillary Clinton and trying to write something insightful and different.

And the schedule can be taxing too: away from home for weeks or months at a time, working non-stop, battling inclement weather and chronic sinus infections. Even the choice of beverage can become a problem. As Christina explained, "You are drinking caffeine all day. So then at night you really need to drink some alcohol if you want to even get four hours of sleep." She referred to this lifestyle as "a gross, grueling existence."

It's important to not get caught up in the celebrity angle of politics either. Christina recommends that the best way to go about this is to always cast a skeptical eye.

She said most politicians truly start out wanting to serve but that their motivations can shift over time.

Don't take things at face value is another tip. Christina suggests starting a sentence with, "We checked into this, and it's actually

[that]" or research why the politician wants a deal to happen and put that in the story too.

"Context is something we forget because we're so busy being fair to both sides," Christina said. She added that young journalists shouldn't "forget you have the brain, and the know-how, and access to information, so you can illuminate this debate in a more substantive way."

She truly believes that journalists sometimes forget they have access to people and places that the general public does not. Doing well with that access will help the media's relationship with the public. "You have the keys to the power. Or at least the keys to *talk* to the power. Use them. Use them wisely, and earn that trust back," she advised.

Christina's experience as a woman in political reporting has been mixed. She told a story of an experience years ago when she was on TV with her friend who happens to be Filipino. They were talking to students, and one asked her friend about being a minority journalist.

Her friend's response, recommending that Christina answer the question first, came as a surprise to her "because it hadn't occurred to me that, as a woman, I would be considered a minority journalist," she explained.

In other instances she believes her gender actually helped her get opportunities where she might not have been the most qualified candidate. She's spent enough time in Washington as one of only two women in a room of 30 white men in navy suits to see the need for minority opportunity. "As somebody who makes hiring decisions, it has become really important to me to help my newsroom look more like America," she said.

She left the White House because *Talking Points Memo*, a liberal blog, recruited her. "It was way more partisan than the conservative paper I had worked for," she acknowledged, comparing it to *The Washington Times.*

Another big change at *Talking Points Memo* was that the entire work process was done virtually. She said that in her time there, not a single piece of paper crossed her desk. Christina jumped into editing at *Roll Call* in 2010. After one year there, she was selected for a competitive semester-long fellowship at Harvard's Institute of Politics, which led to her working at *PBS NewsHour*. She did that for two years. She loved working with people like Judy Woodruff, but in the end she realized, "They wanted a producer, and I didn't know anything about producing television." Her personal life was at a bad point too. "I got divorced in the middle of it," she shared.

Luckily, the bosses at *Roll Call* came calling again, and she took over as editor. That's when everything came full circle in her career. She needed someone on her staff to manage the team covering the House of Representatives. "I kept thinking about my first editor in D.C., the guy who answered the phone when I called from California," she recalled. His name is David Eldridge, and at that point he was still working at *The Washington Times*.

"I ended up hiring him!" she exclaimed. She explained that she knew he'd be good at handling a team of reporters because he had basically taught her everything she knew.

This is one of the proudest moments in her career, and she recounts it to aspiring journalists as an important teaching moment. "You should be kind and courteous to every person you interact with because you never know if they're going to be your boss someday or somebody you're going to need to know," she tells them.

She points to the story of Eric Lesser, who at 22 got his start as a baggage handler for the 2008 Obama presidential campaign and who is now a state senator from Massachusetts. Senator Lesser, who represents the First Hampden and Hampshire district of Massachusetts, 90 miles outside of Boston, was quite impressed with Christina during that campaign.

Lesser's official title was ground logistics coordinator, but Christina is correct in that he was responsible for everyone's baggage, including the 30-odd reporters who traveled on Obama's plane. Lesser described it as, "a little like being the equipment manager for a sports team."

He traveled to 47 U.S. states on that plane, covering 200,000 miles. He explained that Christina traveled on the plane almost as much as he did, and they had a unique relationship because he was a member of the campaign staff and she was a reporter, which required them "to maintain some level of professional distance."

Despite this distance, they were in a high-pressure environment together, and Senator Lesser grew to admire Christina's attitude on the campaign. He notes that she was always the first person to say, "Thank you," and she "really developed a reputation, both among the other reporters and the campaign staff, and Senator Obama himself, as someone who conducted herself with tremendous professionalism and also with great character."

When this interview was initially conducted, Christina had just taken a position as assistant managing editor/politics at the *Los Angeles Times*, a position she took in part so that she and her husband can start a family. "I'm taking myself out of D.C. and the city that I love and this connection to politics. And I'm putting myself in a place I've never lived," she said.

On a final note, when asked what she thinks makes a good political reporter, she said, "You need to be a good listener."

Not focusing on what other people are doing is another bit of advice she shared.

"Put your best mind and your best heart in every question and, hopefully, make some news out of that" was her advice for standing out from the crowd and being true to your audience.

Her passion for politics is as strong as ever. "I care deeply about voting," she said. "I think it's the most important thing that we do. People died for our ability to do that, and I want everyone to feel excited about voting."

Photo credit: Erik M. Lunsford, *St. Louis Post-Dispatch*

Chapter 3

GILBERT BAILON

NOVEMBER 24, 2014, WHEN THE Grand Jury verdict was announced in the case of the shooting of unarmed black teen Michael Brown, there were media trucks and cameras and reporters furiously scribbling notes about their surroundings as far as the eye could see. Many were there for days, weeks even. But few have seen it through since the beginning and have been there to report on every step of the story.

Gilbert Bailon, editor of the *St. Louis Post-Dispatch*, has been. By the time of the Grand Jury verdict, his paper had been solidly covering the events for more than three months. On the day of the verdict that let police officer Darren Wilson walk free, Gilbert estimates that the paper had 15 reporters scattered out in the field. Included in these numbers were staff members in Clayton, which acts as the county seat, and people in Ferguson itself. Plus a handful of photographers to capture the reactions live.

He acknowledged that the safety of his reporters was a priority. Tactics included sending people out in teams of two and making sure staff members were in constant phone communication or were in physical view of one another.

The paper's employees even got a briefing from a SWAT team member in preparation for the coverage. Topics covered included how to interact with the police, what to do if you were injured, and how to react when physically confronted by someone in the crowd.

Despite the preparations, "the threats were real," Gilbert said. Reporters had their phones stolen, some were tear-gassed, and there was one unfortunate incident in which a female staffer was put into a headlock.

The intrepid reporters of the *St. Louis Post-Dispatch* were not deterred. Gilbert and the other editors made it the choice of the individual reporters whether they wanted to be out in the field covering the story. He doesn't recall anyone opting out, instead, they wanted to take advantage of the opportunity. "What I saw more was that people were volunteering; they wanted to be a part of a big story," he explained.

The *Post-Dispatch* reporters out in the field made social media an important part of their strategy. "We didn't just need [social media] from a competitive standpoint," said Gilbert. "We also found that the readers wanted that."

Overall, he is happy with the reliability of their information, confirming that they didn't have any major gaffes. It is always his goal to be fair, balanced and only go with items that can be confirmed. He adheres to the ideal of, "I'd rather be right than be first."

On the night of November 24, 2014 to say that #Ferguson was trending on Twitter is an understatement. Gilbert and his team were busy answering questions from followers like @JaneDueker, who asked if any local media outlets had yet confirmed the decision had been reached. Another of Gilbert's followers stated that the *AP* had confirmed. Rather than potentially mislead one of his readers, Gilbert kept his followers in the know by tweeting back, "No local media is reporting any confirmation and neither is the *Associated Press*."

That social interaction continued throughout that day and the weeks and months that followed. Ferguson actually pushed Gilbert and his team further into becoming "real-time journalists." Gilbert believes all types of events can and should be covered using this approach.

Working in real time has its share of difficulties though. Many witnesses to the shooting said they saw Michael Brown surrender and mouth the words, "Don't shoot!" The accounts were later deemed to be false, but the movement had already spread and that put a lot of pressure on media to report those accounts as fact.

Gilbert and the staff of the *Post-Dispatch* heard from the public when they reported that Michael Brown did not, in fact, have his hands up when he was shot by police officer Darren Wilson.

He explained, "We're not clairvoyant." He continued, "We're for the facts that we do know, based on the information that we can gather from sources that are reliable." He admitted that people are not infallible and can be wrong in certain instances.

At the time of this interview, he recalled that he was recently quite impressed with his reporter Lisa Brown, who live tweeted from a federal courthouse during the trial of former Anheuser-Busch CEOs August Busch III and August Busch IV, who were accused of sexual discrimination. The two members of the Busch family were accused of the discrimination by former lawyer Francine Katz, but a jury later found both men not guilty.

Using social media to cover Ferguson got them thinking, "How can we tell a story in a different way that may not be in print?"

Ferguson did more than get the wheels turning inside the *Post-Dispatch* newsroom; it sparked a massive movement centered around race and abuse of power. Gilbert realized Ferguson went from being a local story to something more when he started receiving calls from people and saw the tweets people posted of Michael Brown's body lying in the street.

It really hit home the first night of the protests, with the looting and the burning of the QuikTrip in Ferguson that Sunday evening, that this was a bigger story. "I don't think initially we thought this was going to trigger a huge national conversation," Gilbert said. "What started here became much bigger," he remarked.

On August 17, 2014, Gilbert appeared on NBC's *Meet the Press* in an episode in which Missouri Governor Jay Nixon was also interviewed. On the program Gilbert was quoted as saying, "This is not unique to Ferguson. I think many, many cities in our region, and many cities throughout the country, have similar issues" with regards to the police brutality issue in the U.S. It is a viewpoint that had been given much more credence in recent months with subsequent protests in cities like Baltimore and Chicago.

Gilbert estimates that some aspect of the Ferguson story was on the front page of the paper every day for many, many months. Some of the readers have since moved past the story, though, and Gilbert has heard from them firsthand. "We're sick of Ferguson. We don't live in Ferguson," he said, recounting common complaints.

Personally, he doesn't always agree. "I don't think we're past the story," Gilbert said in mid-2015. "We think this is a story that's probably going to change a generation of how things are governed." He does concede to a point on the amount of coverage though, "We do need to be measured because people do want to see other stuff now."

Race and police brutality are still very important stories, even if national and international media have mostly moved on from Ferguson. Gilbert acknowledged that the media's images of the situation gave people the impression that "Ferguson is an unsafe place to be." He hopes its citizens now have the opportunity to heal because, as he noted, they are "trying to rebuild."

He brought up Ebola as an example of a similar story that received a lot of national news attention. "We thought the world was ending with Ebola," he said, referencing the first cases of the Ebola virus being found on U.S. soil in Dallas in the fall of 2014. That story has all but disappeared, but, "we kind of lost track of the context," he said. "It's hard to contain that," Gilbert added.

His leadership on the Ferguson series caught the attention of the National Press Foundation, which named Gilbert the 2014 Benjamin C. Bradlee Editor of the Year. The organization selected him because of his ability to clearly cover diversity and the issues of racism in Missouri that were so prevalent in 2014. But this is nothing new to Gilbert. He's long known about the conflicts that can and do stem from racism, and he's made a successful career out of making that known to readers.

Over his 35 years in journalism, Gilbert has often found himself covering minority communities. As a Mexican-American, those opportunities presented themselves early, beginning when he was growing up in Tempe, Arizona, a suburb of Phoenix.

Gilbert was lucky enough to grow up in a household that valued reading and education. His mother, Susan Madrid Jackson, earned a PhD in Reading Education at Arizona State University, where she later taught. She set a good example and kept multiple newspapers around the house. "I was around somebody who was a huge media consumer herself in all forms," he said.

Gilbert attended college at the University of Arizona, graduating in 1981, and later earned a Master's Degree in American History at the University of Texas at Arlington in 1992. His sisters also pursued advanced degrees.

It was his love of reading and writing that drew him to journalism. As a young person he asked himself, "Short of writing books, how do you take that and use it as a vehicle for a career?"

He liked journalism because he liked information. "I liked telling stories, and I was very curious about the world," he added. Interest in becoming an editor came early too. He worked as a student editor at *The Arizona Daily Wildcat* at the University of Arizona between 1980 and 1981, and he soon decided that would be his career path.

After college Gilbert worked at the *Fort Worth Star-Telegram*, *Los Angeles Daily News*, and *The San Diego Union* before finally landing at *The Dallas Morning News* in 1986. He worked there first as a reporter covering immigration and then later as an executive editor and vice president.

As a beginning reporter he was very interested in issues pertaining to his home region, the Southwest. As a Hispanic, Gilbert also has a passion for issues surrounding Mexico and Latin America. In an August 1986 article titled "Area Watchdog

Groups Say Families Torn Apart by Sects' Control of Members," published in *The Dallas Morning News,* he wrote about a woman's adult children who had been lured to Mexico by the religious cult known as Children of God.

Gilbert also wrote a college paper in 1991 that was archived in the UTA library. It's titled *Little Mexico: An Enduring Hub of Mexican Culture in Dallas.* It details the growth of the Dallas neighborhood of Little Mexico, beginning during the Mexican revolution in 1910 and running through the 1980s.

He heavily supports the use of minority voices in news to cover the changing demographics of the U.S. "You need people to be able to tell those stories, find those stories, get the sources that can service them, because nationally, this a huge trend," he said.

He was also integral in the creation of *Al Dia,* a Spanish language offshoot of *The Dallas Morning News,* as founding editor and president. That was in June 2003, less than one year before he was named publisher. "Our mission was to try to educate and inform, to activate people to become informed citizens in the community," he said. At its apex he oversaw a staff of 60.

According to Gilbert, topics covered everything from immigration legalization to how readers could help their children adapt in school as immigrants.

Alfredo Carbajal worked as the managing editor at *Al Dia* during Gilbert's 2003 to 2007 tenure and is now editor. Alfredo said that one of Gilbert's greatest strengths as a journalist is his news judgment. "He's pretty quick at identifying trends and stories outside the usual institutional circles and sources," he said.

Alfredo said that Gilbert makes it a point to empower and motivate people, and this came into play during the early days of *Al Dia.* "We went out and hired dozens of professional journalists to come out to Dallas and start a new venture, and this in itself is exciting," he explained. "But you know the climate of being a startup; it's always the sentiment or feeling that it's different than other things because you're hoping that it's going to reach an audience," Alfredo said. They were in fact trying to reach the underserved Spanish-speaking newspaper readers in Texas.

According to Alfredo, Gilbert's motivation came in the form of a singular vision, "reminding everybody why we were doing what we were doing."

Working in a big market like Dallas was an important learning experience for Gilbert. Nielsen listed the Dallas-Ft. Worth area as the No. 5 television market in 2014-2015, with 2.6 million households, and the No. 6 television market in the Hispanic community for the same time period, with approximately 525,000 households.

When Gilbert moved from Dallas to the smaller metro area of St. Louis, he realized there were elements that have changed over time for markets of all sizes. Gilbert cited two of them: a tightening of resources and a focus on the core area. "It's harder to do some of the stories we used to do because we were in much better touch with people," he said.

Big or small market, he still believes it's important to get out of the office and be visible in the community. "I think that's still a very critical part of our business," he added. In fact he believes that this patience leads to important breakthroughs in the community and leads to some of the strongest stories. "It's always the more difficult stories, the stories that happen over time with people who aren't necessarily trying to seek media attention," said Gilbert. He also noted that you have to have a thick skin. "Not everybody thinks the media is great, and I hear from them every day."

After moving from Texas to Missouri to take the editorial page editor position at the *St. Louis Post-Dispatch* in November 2007, Gilbert was reminded of the importance of using his newspaper staff. "You have a lot of people who have expertise on a lot of issues," he said. "And you rely on them."

This is especially true when it comes to the history of an area. "I have a good idea of what's current, but sometimes I need help with what's history," he explained. Gilbert also believes it's important to be open to asking good questions of his staff and to make sure you broaden your knowledge of the surrounding area as much as possible. "I don't presume I know everything that's going on in the state."

When it comes to his role as an editor, a promotion that was announced in May 2012, Gilbert believes it takes a lot of different abilities. "I think the newspaper editor is setting direction and tone," he said. "And some troubleshooting."

The "direction and tone" includes managing priorities, deciding what to cover and what not to cover, looking at societal issues, and pursuing themes. He also uses his judgment to look at the paper as a whole, look at the headlines, look at the website, and ask himself, "Are we doing the right thing? What's the big story today?"

Another big component of his job is managing people or, as he said, "You're shaping through other people." This includes giving his staff enough leeway to do their jobs well. He said that he personally doesn't post things on the website, but he puts the right people in place and coaches them through the process so that it runs smoothly.

He talked about how a newsroom is full of human beings and that this must be taken into consideration or things will not work out. "Everything you do well or don't do well comes down to our abilities as journalists," Gilbert explained.

Engagement is also one of Gilbert's responsibilities, which includes knowing what is going on in the community, writing a column timed with certain news events, participating in social media, and listening to the readers, who offer both praise and criticism.

A majority of the recent tweets by Gilbert were informative, featuring information about current *Post-Dispatch* articles with direct links to the paper's website. The reporter's Twitter handle was also included in the body of the tweet. On the same day, he tweeted both about the upcoming local fair, and about the group that held the "draw Muhammad" event in Texas, which led to attacks in May 2015, and how the protest group, American Freedom Defense Initiative, had erected 100 billboards in and around St. Louis.

The final component of Gilbert's job is administrative, a role he gladly takes on so "everyone else can focus on the journalism and be really active in digital formats as well as print." The administrative side covers everything from finalizing budgets and hiring to making circulation deadlines and overseeing marketing.

Gilbert has seen the business from two different sides in his long career of working in newspapers. Now that he's an editor, he has a deeper appreciation for the teamwork that goes into putting out the daily paper. "It's been called a daily miracle," Gilbert said. "I still believe that." He credits his reporters with making that happen.

He sees it as his job to make sure they have everything they need to make the daily miracle happen. "It's important that our journalists feel engaged and feel as though they are doing important work." He also tries to give them "room and latitude to maneuver."

Gilbert admits that journalism is "actually harder than ever," due to a reporter's focus being pulled in all of these different directions because of the various social media and multimedia responsibilities.

Even though Gilbert doesn't want his reporters to worry about the revenue aspects of their paper, he still thinks it's important for young journalists to be aware it exists. His advice: "Don't be oblivious to what's happening in our business. It isn't all bad."

When it comes to hiring new reporters, he looks for a few things. The basics are important. "I think the first thing is the ability to read, write, analyze, and put words together," he said. He believes that technical elements can be taught, but most writers are born with an innate ability with words.

He notes that keeping up with current events is important, as is a critical and curious mind with a variety of skills. "I think versatility is really important," he said. For instance, if you're a print reporter, it's good to know how to shoot video, to be versed in basic editing, and have an understanding of photography.

Of his recent hires he points out that the ones who are the most respected come in with "ideas to push us forward," despite their experience or age. He gave examples of recent hires who came in with data-reporting skills, the ability to create really great infographics, and narrative storytelling using videos for the paper's website. "I would tell college students or aspiring people who are even at smaller papers to develop those marketable skills that some of these legacy newsrooms may not have," he commented.

During the months surrounding the shooting of Michael Brown, Gilbert was often asked to speak to the media. Overall this was a good experience, and it taught him a few things. For instance, he believes that it's rare to be flat out misquoted in the press but that the reporter's use of context might be questionable. "It's not incorrect, but it may not have the full framework of what you were trying to say," he explained. He admitted it's moments like this that can challenge him as an editor.

While representing his profession, Gilbert zeroed in on a pet peeve in the way his career field is perceived by the general public. "Probably the biggest beef I have, because this comes up when I speak on panels, is people say 'the media.'" He elaborated, "the media are a huge plural. It's not just the *Post-Dispatch* or professional media outlets trying to provide verified information." He believes that each genre of journalism is truly different, and he genuinely wants to distinguish his paper from those facets of media that have a set agenda and viewpoint.

Overall, the *Post-Dispatch* was lauded for its coverage of the events in Ferguson, and Gilbert's staff photographers were awarded the 2015 Pulitzer Prize for their moving and often heartbreaking images. The award marked the paper's 18th Pulitzer win.

Prior to the Pulitzer Prize announcement, Gilbert acknowledged that everybody wants to win an award, but said, "I don't think that's what's motivating folks." He made it clear that his priority is serving the local community, which has been recently damaged. Noting that is why he got into the business, he said,

"I've only been here [eight] years, but I feel like it's home, and I act like it is."

He did admit that it is nice when journalism that's not on the two coasts is recognized. When they do good work, they hear from readers who encourage them to keep going and keep digging. "That's probably more inspirational than anything I can say," Gilbert said. "Or any award we might win."

Photo credit: Singeli Agnew

Chapter 4

CARRIE LOZANO

BEING UNCOMFORTABLE IS SOMETHING THAT Carrie Lozano believes is inevitable for all journalists. That's because "you'll be uncomfortable for 90 percent of your career."

She's referring to journalists being forced to expose themselves as part of their jobs by inserting themselves into the lives of strangers and often asking personal questions. She would know, since she's been doing that very thing in the award-winning documentaries she's made during the past decade.

Calling loved ones after a death to get information for an obituary, interviewing people who have just experienced a natural disaster, and ambushing people outside the courthouse to get a quote are all part of what Carrie refers to as the "tool box" of what a journalist needs to successfully do their job.

Even if you're uncomfortable, she believes it is important to make the person you're interviewing feel at ease. "Certainly, the second you bring in a camera to any scenario, even if it's not adversarial, it can exponentially complicate the situation," she explained.

She noted that respect is owed to interviewees; make the experience of participation in a documentary the best it can be for them because they give you their time at what is often a vulnerable moment in their lives.

In order to make the interviewee more comfortable, she recommends doing pre-interviews over the phone and spending time with them when the cameras are off. One thing she never does is provide them with the interview questions ahead of the actual interview. Instead she suggests something less extreme: "You can generally tell people what you want to talk about."

These are all skills she has acquired over the years. Her most notable projects include 2002's *The Weather Underground* and 2006's short film *Reporter Zero,* about journalist Randy Shilts, for which she won a Student Academy Award. She called the win "such an honor and a vote of confidence."

It wasn't enough to break down the gender walls that exist in Hollywood though. "The men I know who've won get calls from agents, etc. Me? Nothing," she explained.

Carrie grew up in Whittier, California. Her interest in making documentaries began as an undergraduate at UC Berkeley, where she was initially studying narrative film.

Specifically, three different film classes exposed her to different genres of filmmaking, which eventually led her down the path to documentaries. She took a class in experimental filmmaking from well-known found footage filmmaker, Craig Baldwin, who gave "shocking" critiques on students' work like "that was so boring!" Moving image artist Ernie Gehr taught her about avant-garde films, and he drove her to make her own, hand-processed 8 mm films, which were screened at local theaters. Finally, Kathy Geritz, longtime curator of the Pacific Film Archive, taught a history of documentary film course "that really captured my imagination," Carrie said.

Although she appreciates documentaries as art just as much, she believes that journalistic standards apply to documentary filmmaking. She quotes her friend and mentor, Jon Else, known for acclaimed documentaries like *Eyes on the Prize: America's Civil Rights Years,* when stating that, "Whatever the audience believes to be true, needs to be true."

Robert Greene, filmmaker-in-chief of the Jonathan B. Murray Center for Documentary Journalism at the University of Missouri, brings a slightly different perspective to the table. He has directed five feature-length documentaries, and in his view, he doesn't think "either [journalism or film] should be subservient to the other."

He believes that documentaries should be guided by the pillars of journalism, "which to me are ethics and honesty and truth, even if objective truth is impossible."

Subjectivity, too, is impossible to get around, especially once staging and recreation become part of the mix, he said. But documentary filmmakers are entitled to take those creative liberties—as he did in his 2014 film *Actress* when he recreated a pivotal scene—one that did occur in real life, he said.

It goes both ways too, Robert said. "By the same token, I think journalism could use more cinema, could use more subtlety and irony and ambiguity in the way it's presented."

The best way to create a credible documentary is starting with reliable sources, something that Carrie takes very seriously. If she ever had reason to believe the subject wasn't being truthful, she said, "I don't think it's usable."

This doesn't mean that all documentary footage must be figuratively viewed as black or white; she acknowledged there is usually room for ambiguity. "Real life is not that clean," she said, "so my approach is usually to just embrace it and be transparent with the viewer."

Another one of her documentarian friends, Dan Krauss, referred to this process as "your contract with the audience."

In Carrie's view all of this is for naught if you don't have the single most important tenet of all good films: a story. According to her, elements like a story arc and great interview subjects who are willing to go on the record must be part of the equation. She doesn't discount the importance of visuals either, which she referred to as "something is happening in front of the camera, not just people talking."

She stated that if you have an incredible story, there is always a way to visualize it, to tell it.

However, having a good story isn't a surefire fix-all if the filmmaker doesn't have the key personality traits to make themselves a success. Carrie sees persistence as the most important trait. She acknowledged that talent, passion and intelligence are all factors too, but consistency is what helps people rise above.

"The people I see who are really successful in journalism are just dogged," she said. "They can go through the emotional roller coaster of this field and still wake up every day and still be motivated to tell a story and be obsessed with the subject matter."

One of the main reasons persistence is such a necessity is because of the sheer number of times documentary filmmakers will face rejection, especially when it involves finances. Carrie said that overall the industry has limited funds for independent filmmakers. She pointed out that there are more filmmakers than funds or outlets for these films. "It's a very competitive, difficult, difficult market."

Some documentary filmmakers even allow cable television channels to use their films for free in exchange for other types of compensation. In an article titled "Locating the Sweet Spot: What Will TV Channels Pay for Your Doc?" James Ackerman, CEO of The Documentary Channel, told writer Peter Hamilton that his channel licensed certain films for free and paid with exposure, publicity for awards, and by completing a portion of their funding requirements stipulated by the film's investors.

Despite the competition in the market and lack of funds, Carrie does not advise filmmakers to give away their work for free on sites like YouTube in order to get their stuff noticed. She added that she doesn't do it personally and doesn't believe it is practical.

What she advised instead is to "develop a marketable skill." She cited side jobs like editing corporate videos and being hired as the cinematographer on bigger budget projects to pay the bills, as good examples. Academy Award-winning filmmaker Errol Morris, who shoots commercials in between personal projects, was a person she mentioned as an example. In an archived March 2015 interview with the now-defunct website Grantland, Errol said, "Commercials saved my ass."

Carrie doesn't believe making documentary films is for the lighthearted either. That go-getter attitude is needed to persevere when the going gets tough. "It's complicated work," she said. "I think there are certain parts of it that are really fun, but I just don't feel like anything is really easy, to be honest with you."

Coincidentally, believing in your cause despite it being perceived as radical is the theme of both of Carrie's two most well-known films. The 2002 film *The Weather Underground*, on which Carrie acted as producer, covers the aggressive offshoot of the 1960s and 1970s group Students for a Democratic Society.

Members of the Weather Underground had the goal of overthrowing the government, and they facilitated this goal by placing bombs in highly trafficked areas, including the Pentagon, the U.S. Capitol, and various locations throughout New York City.

The film came out not long after the tragic events of September 11, 2001, and just prior to the invasion of Iraq. Carrie was surprised by the film's positive reception. "I like to think it's because it's a good film, but I think a lot of it was just a very, very particular political moment that we were in," she explained.

Reporter Zero is a short film about the life and career of controversial journalist Randy Shilts, who was a national correspondent with the *San Francisco Chronicle*. Headquartered in one of the hotbeds of the AIDS crisis, he is best known for his 1987 book, *And the Band Played On: Politics, People, and the AIDS Epidemic.*

At more than 600 pages, it's a chronicle of the early days of the disease and crisis, and it is unapologetic of its criticism of then-President Ronald Reagan and what many saw as his refusal to confront the problem head on due to AIDS being classified as a "gay disease."

Journalists are forever taught to be impartial, but Carrie found that was one of the great things about Randy Shilts. "I think to me Randy's significance was that he wasn't neutral," she said. "Letting gay people die of AIDS is not a neutral thing." She added that Randy saw the media's role as watchdog and that his legacy was that he did take an official stand, and really tried to right a wrong.

After all these years, the topic of fighting AIDS has stayed near and dear to Carrie. She helped produce *The Ballad of Fred*

Hersch, a documentary about the composer and pianist who was the first openly gay jazz musician and who survived a two-month AIDS-related coma.

Carrie wrapped the feature-length film shortly after leaving her position at Al Jazeera America, the satellite television channel dedicated to Arabic news. Her departure came less than a year before the network announced it would halt its American operations in April 2016 and 700 jobs would be lost. Reflecting on the news, she acknowledged that the network had "serious issues," but she still considered it a highlight of her career.

"It was ill-conceived given the digital landscape and decline of appointment television. But I'm sorry to see it go," Carrie said. "We're losing an important voice and perspective on the airwaves, which I hope they reinvigorate in the digital realm."

In her nearly two years with the organization, she was the senior producer of *Fault Lines,* a position she described as akin to a managing editor in a print newsroom, before she became executive producer of documentaries.

As described on the company's website, "*Fault Lines* takes you beyond the headlines and holds the powerful to account as we examine the U.S.'s role in the world."

Recent episodes focused on issues like the plight of migrant farm workers, Baltimore's history of police brutality, and the U.S. role in South Sudan's civil unrest. Carrie was impressed with the organization's commitment to diversity, noting that it was a "core value" there, instead of something they merely pay lip service to.

In addition she felt that her treatment there as a female of color was top notch. "I actually never felt more supported in my career than I did there in a lot of ways," she said.

Working on the *Fault Lines* program was an equally rewarding experience. She described their commitment to excellence in all areas like cinematography and the reporting to putting "the premium on everything."

One piece she was particularly proud of was "Haiti in a Time of Cholera," a piece reported on by correspondent Sebastian Walker which won an Emmy as well as a Peabody. It was a follow up to a previous piece titled "Haiti Six Months On."

Carrie complimented Sebastian when talking about working alongside him on this episode because he had been living in Haiti after the earthquake and reporting from the ground for many months. "He knew almost in his sleep how to put that together," she said, referring to the 25-minute program.

Other notable stories on *Fault Lines* include the team's coverage of Ferguson, bail bonds, opioid addiction, and domestic homicide. She always thought, in terms of documentary TV programs, "*Fault Lines* was ahead of the game."

Carrie is a fan of the new visual style of documentary film-making that usually includes some type of moving graphics or animation. In fact she mentioned that, acting as executive producer, she is currently in development on a film with Bernardo Ruiz that will be heavily animated.

She explained how, for a long time, this type of work was prohibited by cost, but now it is available to almost anyone. She does caution against it becoming a standard in the industry for a multitude of reasons, especially, "if you're doing recreations but you're not telling [the audience] they're recreations." She draws the line at tricking the audience, but nonetheless she believes this is an exciting time in filmmaking.

Carrie has very specific views on editing. It's her belief that editors should study story structure so they understand why something works or doesn't work. She also explained that the invisible flow of the story is important so that the viewer doesn't realize they are moving forward in time.

Reveals are also a key element in Carrie's editing tool bag. She equated these edits to the classic infomercial trope of "But wait, there's more!" Or as she put it, "You should surprise the viewer and take them to unexpected places."

Carrie doesn't always get the chance to produce and direct her dream projects. In particular she regrets she wasn't able to make the definitive film on noted novelist James Baldwin, who wrote the 1953 book *Go Tell It On The Mountain* and the popular 1955 collection of essays *Notes of a Native Son*. An 87-minute episode of television program *American Masters* profiled James Baldwin in 1989 and was directed by Karen Thorsen.

Carrie pointed out that you might not always be interested in a documentary subject when it is presented to you on paper, but if it's well told, "it will grab you and you'll have an experience that you didn't expect."

As far as who grabs Carrie's attention, she has been incredibly impressed by documentarian Joshua Oppenheimer. "I think he's brilliant. His artistry and creativity amaze me. He has taken the form to new levels," she said. His 2014 BAFTA-winning film, *The Act of Killing,* is an example that showcases his unique style, as it challenges former members of Indonesian death squads to recreate their famous mass killings in the cinematic genre of their choice.

Carrie's adopted home, the San Francisco Bay Area, is rife with talented filmmakers. The area may be best known as the filmmaking base of both George Lucas and Francis Ford Coppola. Both still work and reside in the area, but more recent success stories include David Fincher of *Gone Girl* and *House of Cards* fame, and Ryan Coogler, an Oakland native, who directed the 2013 Sundance Film Festival Grand Jury Prize-winning film, *Fruitvale Station* and most recently brought *Creed,* the newest installment in the *Rocky* saga, to the big screen.

Carrie said that this community is partially why she stayed in the area after graduating from UC Berkeley's undergrad program in 1996 and grad school in 2005. She acknowledged that there is actually more paid work in New York and that it in fact might be a better place for her career, but in the end the Bay Area is for her long-term.

"It would be hard to imagine leaving it," she said.

Photo credit: Jared Harrell, BuzzFeed News

Chapter 5

KENDALL TAGGART

KENDALL TAGGART MIGHT BE A Millennial working at one of the most famous news media outlets, but she's not afraid to take an old school approach when it comes to her reporting.

For one of her most recent series with BuzzFeed, she and fellow reporter Alex Campbell sent out public records requests, scoured through jail logs, showed up at courthouses unannounced to speak with judges, and even went knocking on dozens of doors in Texas to see if they might get to chat with a teenager skipping school.

Kendall's assignment was to investigate truancy laws in Texas. She and her reporting partner dedicated nearly six months to the series. "Our editor—I don't know if it's a habit of his or not, since I haven't been at BuzzFeed very long—but he basically set a mandate: 'by the end of the year, I want you to pitch me the most ambitious investigative series you can.'"

That was back in December 2014, when Kendall was new to the company and looking for her first piece. She had come across an article about a judge in Maryland who was fining kids, a "profile of this sort of tough-love judge," as she described it.

"The idea of fining kids sort of struck us as something neither of us had been aware of before ... That got us talking to a lot of different juvenile justice experts around the country, former judges, and asking if [they know of] anywhere this happens a lot."

Their response was: Texas.

The word on Texas was that legislators had taken truancy laws a little too far. Laws that were put in place to protect minors by keeping them in school were landing them in jail.

In a matter of weeks, Kendall had a database filled with hundreds of truancy cases in that state. She dug through records in 10 counties across Texas and soon discovered that at least a thousand students had skipped school in the past three years—and gone to jail for it. And that finding just scratched the surface.

There are more than 250 counties in Texas, so Kendall knew they couldn't include all of them. "Every time we added a new place or county to look at, it became this whole additional reporting mission ... We knew we couldn't do the universe. We just picked something that felt like it would give us a sense of what was going on, even though we knew it would be incomplete."

Kendall was fortunate enough to be afforded the luxury of time to spend on one story, but she still faced a pretty big deadline. She and Alex wanted to complete the story in time for legislators to consider policy reform.

The series began to appear on BuzzFeed's website on April 22, 2015. This gave them about a month for Texas lawmakers to respond or take action on any of the 20 truancy-related bills that had been introduced in 2015.

"There's been a lot of last minute politics," Kendall said in the final days of the legislative session. "They hold legislative sessions every two years for six months. It's this mad rush to try to get dozens of bills through."

The stories certainly made their rounds. Five days after BuzzFeed ran the initial story, at least one school district in Texas suspended its truancy policies.

Reading the BuzzFeed story outraged some lawmakers because many of them weren't aware of the magnitude of the situation. Even a Houston state representative who authored a bill that would decriminalize truancy was shocked by the numbers. "You've gotta be kidding me," said Democrat Harold Dutton, Jr.

after the initial story ran online.

Another lawmaker went so far as to promise to print out copies of the article to take with him into the legislative session. "I'm gonna personally hand one to every senator today and ask them to read it," Texan Democratic Senator John Whitmire told BuzzFeed during the final week of the legislative session of 2015.

Don Coffey, a judge in Harris County, Texas, admitted that sending kids to jail while making them miss additional days of school is counter-productive. "It's totally against the whole spirit of what I think the law should be," he told BuzzFeed.

One of the elements that made the story so compelling was that Kendall had identified a student who had skipped school and landed herself in jail—for nine days. After her sentence, administrators informed the then 17-year old that she was to be kicked out of school.

Serena Vela was a junior in high school when she was charged in a criminal court that sent her to spend time in an adult prison. She shared a cell with two other women and "mostly slept" and "did her best to stave off boredom."

Other students in the article claimed adult inmates were seen "beating each other and soliciting sex."

Serena was the main subject of the BuzzFeed story, but several other students and their parents were interviewed for the series. Identifying the kids who had been jailed in Texas on truancy charges was relatively simple: it was all a matter of public record.

"We started with a list of probably 100 kids, people under 18, who we could see had been in jail for this. Alex and I started Facebook messaging as many as we could find. But pretty quickly we realized we weren't getting responses." Even still, messaging through Facebook was the reporters' best bet since "some of [the kids] have really common names, and most aren't really in public records otherwise. They're too young to have a voting record or some of the other ways we might find people."

Kendall and Alex first took a trip to Texas back in early 2015, but their first interview wasn't with the kids. They met with Judge

John Payton, who had jailed 66 kids for truancy in 2014 alone. "We just showed up at his courthouse, and it ended up working out," Kendall said. That was the first of five trips made by the two reporters, so each trip had to count.

Between the interviews and the comprehensive data, the story had fallen into place somewhat seamlessly. But there's a reason certain stories get more treatment than others: the piece required time. Not only did Kendall need to piece together points of data she found in the jail logs, she also needed to come up with the faces like Serena's that create an anecdotal storyline and paint a vivid picture for readers.

After Kendall and Alex interviewed the judge, they went knocking on doors around the suburbs of Dallas.

Before finding Serena, there was another person they had envisioned using as the main subject for the story. "We found a great character right outside Dallas ... In the end her story didn't check out with any of the public records we could get. I don't know if that's because the jail records were wrong or not, but she had told us a lot of really terrible things that had happened to her while she was in jail, and we couldn't verify some of the basic details."

When that person fell through, Kendall and Alex made the four-hour drive to Houston. Kendall said they lucked out that their editors had planned extra days for the first Texas trip, with the expectation the reporters might need more time when they were on the ground.

Once they arrived in Houston, they knocked on about 30 doors before connecting with Serena. "There was one day where we had 15 doors and couldn't find anyone at home. And none of the handwritten notes we left generated any responses. We were feeling a bit demoralized, and one of the last houses we knocked on was this pretty run-down trailer ... There weren't any lights on, and we were kind of sloshing through the mud in front of her house."

To Kendall's astonishment Serena's little brother answered the door and gave out his mom's phone number. The next day Kendall and Alex met Serena at her work to talk. (They also interviewed her boss, who said she had never skipped work).

"She's got a lot more pressing concerns in her life than helping reporters go and get her court records, which are sealed to people like us. There was a lot of back and forth, and Alex ended up hopping back on a plane to get some of that stuff tracked down when we couldn't get it during the first visit."

Under state law in Texas, you're an adult at 17, at least for criminal purposes. "There's some wiggle room, but our editor felt pretty strongly that anyone under 18 needed to talk to their parents first," Kendall said. Fortunately, Serena was over 18 at the time of the interview, so there was no issue with getting parental consent to interview her. Plus her mother herself participated in an interview.

Even for a quiet teen, Serena was forthcoming when it came to detailing her experience. Serena's mom was a willing participant in the story, but she drew a line when it came to certain topics. For instance, as the BuzzFeed investigation pointed out, kids who skipped school were often fined. The problem was that most kids or their families couldn't afford to pay those fines, which is what landed them behind bars.

So Kendall looked for ways to illustrate that Serena's family didn't have a lot of spare cash to pay for fines that amounted to $2,700, in at least one instance. "I remember asking her mom, 'How much do you pay in rent?' She was like, 'What the hell does that matter?' These aren't the kinds of things that people are proud of sharing, it's an awkward thing to do," Kendall said. "When her mom didn't want to tell us how much she paid in rent, that seemed like a fair thing to want to keep private. We just talked with them about how they spent their days and the other parts of their life that could help us paint that picture more clearly for the readers. We didn't touch the things that didn't seem necessary."

On June 19, 2015, Texas Governor Greg Abbott signed the bill into law that would stop jailing kids for skipping school. So the

BuzzFeed investigation had a clear-cut impact on the state's laws. "I feel good," Kendall said, following the news that the governor sided with her story, "but also feel like we were a small piece of a larger puzzle that made this happen."

This isn't the first time Kendall's work has gained national attention. Prior to joining BuzzFeed in October 2014, she spent more than four years with The Center for Investigative Reporting (CIR) in Emeryville, California. She worked with the team that exposed faulty construction of California public schools and was a Pulitzer finalist for local reporting in 2012 for the series "On Shaky Ground." Later in her time with the CIR, Kendall won a Barlett and Steele award for her investigation on "America's Worst Charities." The award is given annually to innovative investigative reporters by the Donald W. Reynolds National Center for Business Journalism.

The Neiman Foundation also named her and her reporting partner finalists for the Taylor Family Award for Fairness in Journalism for the series on which she collaborated with Kris Hundley from the *Tampa Bay Times*. The story looked at thousands of charities in the U.S. and identified the 50 charities that spent the least amount on the cause for which they fundraise.

The story came about in a somewhat unconventional way for the CIR, Kendall said. She recalled that her editor, Mark Katches, mentioned a story he'd investigated years earlier for *The Orange County Register* when three different charities—raising funds for firefighters, cancer, and terminally ill children—were all operating out of one house in Southern California.

"He noticed this and thought it was weird," Kendall said. "In the end [his] story ended up resulting in a federal investigation that sent people to federal prison for charity fraud ... I think he always had that in the back of his mind that there's got to be a systemic story about how no one is watching and making sure this stuff doesn't happen."

Essentially, Kendall was instructed to collect the data to determine how often fraudulent charities were operating. She found herself starting at the California Attorney General's office, which gathers data from telemarketers.

The first charity that caught Kendall's eye was Kids Wish Network. The nonprofit was repeatedly spending 80 to 90 cents of every dollar on fundraising (versus programs for the non-profit's mission), and it was raising millions, Kendall was quick to point out. Kids Wish Network was based in Holiday, Florida. "That happened to be in the backyard of the *Tampa Bay Times*," Kendall said.

Mark knew the editor, Chris Davis, from the Investigative Reporters and Editors (IRE) world, so he reached out to see if he wanted to collaborate on the project and whether he had someone on his team who would work on this story with The Center for Investigative Reporting. Both media outlets knew this couldn't be the only place charity fraud was rampant. The editors asked, "How can we do a bigger story?"

And so the ambitious project was born. It lasted for 18 months, and from day one Kendall and Kris Hundley were partners—even if they were working from opposite sides of the country.

The scenario was unusual, according to Kendall, because most of the CIR's stories are usually further developed before the organization brings in another media outlet as a partner, or at least that's how it worked when Kendall was there. CNN, for example, often jumps into projects such as "America's Worst Charities" later in the game to add video elements to stories.

Kendall acknowledged there is a somewhat different model now because the CIR has a broader online following than before. It launched Reveal, its new website, and a podcast, among other initiatives, to build the brand.

"When I was there, CIR didn't have a huge following of its own. It was publishing a dozen major investigations in a year but about all sorts of different topics. There wasn't really a core group of readers who were coming back. Partnerships were a way to get the story seen, in part."

The CIR's director of distribution and engagement, Meghann Farnsworth, explained that it operates under an adapted model nowadays. The organization has bolstered its lean staff of nearly 25 employees from when Kendall first started in 2010 to close to 70 employees today.

"With investigative reporting, a lot of news organizations have taken a hit. It's a difficult thing to do," Farnsworth said. "I think our management has been visionary about how we can grow and where the industry is going.

"We still do a lot of great partnerships, and now, with the radio show, more copy is going just to our website. We're not in competition with other news organizations, because we just don't have the same kind of content. But we do need to build up a brand for ourselves, and that means having some exclusive content that's just for us."

Even if the CIR doesn't consider itself to be a direct competitor to mainstream media, Kendall described how it could get competitive and even uncomfortable in certain situations. "It was often hard to get newspapers to carve out a lot of space in print for something they didn't feel ownership of," she said.

Outside news outlets would sometimes be willing to run close to 1,000 words, but Kendall said that was a huge sacrifice, considering the CIR's reporters had spent months on these complex, lengthy investigations.

Other times, she said, it was a matter of not knowing whose toes you might be stepping on. "If you have a great investigation about a criminal justice issue, the cops reporter at that paper might be less than thrilled about the fact that some outsider is coming in."

And having too many editors can sometimes create division among the team. "Sometimes people would have different opinions about what the crux of the story should be, and that could be really hard to navigate, especially if people aren't working in the same building. They're working from across the country."

Kendall said her partnership with the *Tampa Bay Times* wasn't so much of a challenge in that aspect, because it was an equal undertaking for both parties, and all parties were involved from the beginning.

In general Kendall and Kris co-reported from separate coasts — Kendall in California and Kris in Florida.

The first time they met was in Kansas City, Missouri, two hours before they went in to interview the attorney who represented most of the charities the reporters ultimately identified and wrote about. "We often ended up meeting or hanging out that way. We met up in Iowa, in Michigan. We'd hop on a plane and end up wherever we needed to do our reporting."

Kendall started her reporting on nonprofits with public documents, but surprisingly, they weren't the Form 990s, the financial reports filed annually with the Internal Revenue Service by nonprofit organizations. They did use information from the 990s but not as their main source of data.

"I didn't realize it when we first got into this, but the IRS does very little to regulate charities," she said, noting that state attorneys general or secretaries of state have the authority to go after any charity that's raising money in their state. That means if it's a New York charity, and they raise money from California, the California Attorney General can take action.

So they went to the biggest states first and requested paperwork from the ones that require charities to file there. Kendall explained that each state requires telemarketers and direct-mail companies to fill out a form that tells how much money they raised for charity that year and how much actually went to the charity.

Another useful tool was the audited financial statement that many charities must file. "Those can sometimes be more helpful than the 990. They'll tell you things about family relationships and other conflicts of interest that might be involved," she said.

And then in other states Kendall and Kris looked at lists of telemarketing companies that are required to register in those states. The forms included employee names, addresses, and other contact information.

"For some of our reporting, from those lists of employees we could try to figure out who was a former employee and then call them to ask about how that company works and what kinds of charities they made calls for."

The 990s came in handy also, but because the IRS does not yet publish PDFs with searchable entries, it took Kendall about three weeks to manually input data entries to get the information into a format they could use online. "It was a bit of a headache," she said.

While many records came from California, not all of the charities' information was available there. To look at each of the other states, Kendall turned to the National Association of State Charity Officials, or NASCO. "More often than not they have more documents than what's listed online, if you file a public records request or ask nicely," she said.

The "ask nicely" token was key for a project like this, which involved thousands of pages of records. As Kendall tells it, the team didn't pay for any records used in the entire project. "In general there was a culture at The Center for Investigative Reporting for not paying for records—not to be cheapskates, but it was sort of ethical, like 'these are public records that we've already paid for in taxes. We shouldn't have to repay for them.'"

Sometimes, in order to avoid paying for records, the CIR had to compromise. One time Kendall flew to the Illinois Attorney General's office in Chicago, where they put 16 boxes in one room and told her to make the copies herself. That's not surprising, and it's only natural for investigative reporters to get backlash from certain agencies, Kendall said. "I think our role as investigative reporters is generally to uncover information that no one wants made public," she said.

The approach might sound skeptical to some, but she said, "That's sort of the beat of an investigative reporter." For instance, after the series went live, Kendall and the editorial team often heard the question: "Why not 'America's *Best* Charities?'"

"Charities doing great work certainly deserve attention, but I think there *is* coverage of that. You could argue there should be more," she acknowledged.

Once Kendall and Kris had the documents they needed, they essentially compared each charity to identify which paid the highest percentage of expenses for professional fundraising, coupled with which ones paid the most for overhead costs.

That's another reason the CIR and the *Tampa Bay Times* didn't reverse the methodology and name the best charities. "The reporting we needed to find bad charities ... I don't think it equipped us well or gave us a roadmap for how we would find good ones. A charity that spends zero dollars on overhead is probably a mess," she said.

Charity Navigator and GiveWell are a couple of the resources Kendall named for people to learn which charities are in fact most effective.

Aside from the documents themselves, one of Kendall's and Kris' trips was dedicated to interviewing Errol Copilevitz, the attorney who worked on behalf of the charities in question. The interview eventually turned into the third part of the series that ran in 2013. Kendall said he was one of the first people they contacted before they became too involved with the reporting on the charities.

It was important to Kendall that Copilevitz not feel that the reporters were coming in with any preconceived understandings, and without having to call the bulk of his clients before he was able to share his side of the story. "I think if we'd gone six months later to interview him, and he already felt our story was focusing on charities he didn't think deserved attention, I doubt he would have said yes," Kendall said. "At some point he did shut off and would only talk to us through an attorney."

At that point Kendall and Kris dealt with the minor factual questions they needed to clarify through written questions they sent to him. "We already had a good sense of what kind of guy he was in his more off-the-cuff answers to the things we needed to know," she said.

Kendall didn't want to ambush him, and that goes for any interview she has after investigating that person or company for months upon months. "I would go in early with people. Don't wait until you think you've got them or something like that," she advised. "Going to people when they feel you're still there to listen, as opposed to after you've done all your reporting and telling them this is just a courtesy call, makes a big difference."

Eighteen months of research meant thousands of pages of documents and interviews with dozens of people. Piecing those two together was quite the process. "When it got towards the end, and we were doing really close edits of the project, I flew to St. Petersburg (Florida) and twice spent about a week there to work next to [Kris] so that we could finish it up. My editor from California, Mark, came out as well. At the end we locked ourselves in an office for 48 hours to just read every word, but for the most part the work was done separately."

After the series was published, the CIR and the *Tampa Bay Times* had a lot of attention come their way between the awards and recognition the reporters received. "This was certainly more attention than I've ever received for a story," Kendall said.

Even two years later, just two weeks after Kendall's truancy story ran on BuzzFeed, she garnered more attention for the charities series. The Federal Trade Commission filed a lawsuit against four charities in May 2015. The suit charged them with not spending enough on their causes. The charities were fined millions of dollars and each dissolved within 24 hours of the announced investigation filed on behalf of the FTC and all 50 states.

One of the four charities had been named in Kendall's series. In fact her work was cited by *The New York Times* when the FTC announced its investigation, although she's certainly not taking credit for the commission's action by any means. "I think some-times it feels like the way we measure the impact of stories is not as clear cut as we'd like it to be," Kendall added.

Back at the start of her investigation, Kendall had "heard grumblings" that the state attorneys general were interested in this group of cancer charities, although the reporters didn't have any other details since the FTC's blanket statement is that it can "neither confirm or deny" an ongoing investigation.

"We did our reporting separately from that and came across some things the state regulators hadn't been aware of. But—to some degree—they were already on it before we started writing about it," Kendall said. Regardless, Kendall said, she was glad to play a part in such a huge investigation.

At both the CIR and BuzzFeed, Kendall has been able to spend several months at a time on a project. And she knows she's lucky to have had that privilege. She knows that the norm at many pub-lications is to "squeeze in half a day a week on the side, although I know some reporters who start out pitching a story that might take a month. The next time they do a story, it might be a two-month process. Then they incrementally get their way up there, gain enough credibility with the editors. It's such an expensive thing to do, I think, for any news operation."

Spending that much time on a single piece creates a tremen-dous amount of pressure, Kendall said. "The one thing I love and hate about the long-term projects is every day that goes by, the story had better get better. Once you hit Day 100 at least, you had better know it's going to pan out. You can't go to your editor and say, 'You know, I don't think there's anything here.' He'd tell you, 'You should have told me that three months ago.'

"There are days, even three months in, when you feel like 'maybe everything we thought was true isn't,' because you've just learned something that changes the story. That's the scary part about long-term projects that sometimes makes me want to write more regularly."

But Kendall wouldn't go as far as to say she wants to work on breaking news on a daily basis. Both styles of reporting have their pros and cons. "I think I would have a hard time doing breaking news reporting," she said. "It's an amazing skill. I watch people do it every day at BuzzFeed now. But I tend to second guess, and I wonder about the five things I don't know about the topic, and I have to track those down first before I'm confident in writing the one paragraph we need for the story. That would make me a really atrocious breaking news reporter."

Photo credit: courtesy of Joan Ryan (pictured, left)

Chapter 6

JOAN RYAN

AT JOAN RYAN'S VERY FIRST newspaper job, she'd been referred to as "a little gal on the *Sentinel* desk who was maybe talking about writing sports." Approximately 15 years later, she changed fans' perspectives of gymnastics and revealed hard truths about one of the most popular Olympic sports.

Her stint as a journalist didn't carry her through retirement, but there's no doubt her work made a significant impact on sports journalism. Books were published and movies were created based on her thorough sports coverage.

She first showed an interest in journalism in high school, and despite being editor of the school's paper, she never considered moving forward with it. "I never said, 'Oh, I'm going to grow up and be a journalist.'"

A self-proclaimed introvert, at that point journalism was simply a way for her to feed her intense curiosity about other people's lives. Working at the newspaper allowed her the entrée to "talk to people I wouldn't normally have the nerve to."

Joan started her collegiate career at the University of Florida in Gainesville as a building construction major. The topic quickly bored her, and she lasted a semester before switching to journalism. She may have been studying journalism at Florida, but she felt too "self-conscious" to get a position on the school paper, *The Independent Florida Alligator*, particularly because of its esteemed reputation.

Her original intent was to be an editor, which also played into her lack of confidence and tendency to be shy. The editing role appealed to her since she "was going to be inside — where you still get all this unbelievable information, and you're reading all of these great stories," as she described it.

The timing couldn't have been more perfect to get a job in editing, thanks in part to two superstar journalists in Washington, D.C. who made investigative reporting truly sexy when they broke one of the biggest stories in American history: Watergate. "When I graduated in 1981, post Woodward and Bernstein, nobody coming out of college wanted to be an editor," she said. "So I had a really easy time getting a job."

Joan's first job was at the *Orlando Sentinel* as an editor working on the "Little Sentinel" section. She soon realized that she needed to get some writing experience, because "that's the heart and soul of a newspaper." Luckily, that's when she first came in contact with then editor David Burgin.

It was a good match because she grew up reading the newspaper and soon realized that "the most lively stories, the most fun stories, were in the sports section."

One of six kids in an Irish-Catholic family, who spent half her childhood in Ridgewood, New Jersey, and the other half in Plantation, Florida, playing sports was a way for Joan to bond with her father; specifically, on the diamond with the daughters in the family playing softball and the sons playing baseball.

One of her first struggles as a reporter took place while covering a professional football game of the Orlando Renegades. The Renegades were part of the United States Football League, the upstart competitor to the National Football League. The USFL was created by David Dixon and the first games were played in the spring of 1983.

In this particular game, the Renegades were playing the Birmingham Stallions out of Alabama, and Joan had been assigned to write a sidebar on the visiting team, which she described as "the lowest rung of reporting."

By halftime she had determined that her sidebar item would

cover the injury sustained by Joe Cribbs, a former NFL player with the Buffalo Bills, who was the star of the Stallions. At halftime she asked their PR person if Cribbs would be available outside the locker room after the game. She was told no and that she would have to cover the story from inside the locker room just like any male reporter.

As she remembers it she had been in the Tampa Bay Buccaneers' locker room a few times while covering local NFL games, but that was a less daunting prospect because "there were so many people that you could kind of just blend in."

She walked into the Stallions locker room, and it was nearly empty because they were the visiting team. She described that the players and coaches registered for a beat of silence that she was standing there, and "then it just erupted in this sort of playground bullying, remarks, teasing" that left her "absolutely mortified and embarrassed." She composed herself, knowing that she was on deadline and needed to speak to Joe Cribbs.

Standing in front of a locker was a player bent over, using a long-handled razor to cut off the tape that football players wear around their ankles and wrists. Joan was wearing a skirt that day, and before she realized what was happening, "I feel the handle of the razor going up my leg, towards the hem of my skirt." To this day, she's unsure what he was trying to do to her, but, understandably, it made her uncomfortable. She doesn't remember what she said because "you kind of blackout in situations where you are just so overwhelmed," but she *does* remember turning towards the door.

On her way out she spotted a man wearing a red V-neck sweater, the attire reserved for the team's coaches, laughing at her. She was shocked to see someone in charge of the team enjoying the spectacle.

She left the locker room, found the PR guy, and told him to find Joe Cribbs so that she could complete her interview. He did, but "I'm sure I asked him some bad questions, and he gave me bad answers and I went out and wrote my bad story." Later, while looking through the media guide, she realized that the man in the red V-neck sweater was the owner of the team. "I thought, 'Wow, that's a good tone to set! What a grown-up.'"

The sports editor and the editor of the *Orlando Sentinel* filed a formal complaint with the USFL. The league folded in 1985 due to unrelated reasons, most of which were financial.

She was asked if this incident changed her professional attire at all, but it turned out she rarely wore skirts leading up to that day in the Stallions locker room. "I almost always wore slacks. I don't remember making a conscious decision to stop wearing skirts," she said.

Not everything that came out of this situation was bad though; in fact it drove her to continue covering sports. The situation in the Stallions locker room made her see how much the players and the hierarchy of the USFL, which she saw as "representing sports in general," really didn't want her around. "And that's the moment I really, really wanted to be a sports writer," she said. "I'm not leaving. You're not chasing me away and you're not chasing women away."

Melissa Ludtke was a sports journalist covering baseball for *Sports Illustrated* in 1977 when she was denied access to the locker rooms by then Major League Baseball Commissioner Bowie Kuhn. Her employer filed a lawsuit, *Ludtke and Time Inc. v. Kuhn*, that same year. A federal judge ruled in her favor, and she was given equal access to the teams' locker rooms—a place that the Los Angeles Dodgers had previously voted that she could enter before Kuhn denied her that access.

Melissa spent time in locker rooms during her career as a sports reporter and viewed being there as an anthropologist might. "You had to understand the locker room culture as you went in," she explained. "And you had to be around it enough in non-threatening ways in order to absorb how the guys treated each other."

Seeking to understand how players interacted with each other helped to give her a context for how they acted with her and

Melissa acknowledged that "on top of that there always had to be in your own mind a line that couldn't be crossed." The type of line that was crossed against Joan when she walked into the Stallions' locker room that day in 1983.

For Joan Ryan, being a woman in a male-dominated industry did have some perks. To start with, the male sports reporters who made up her pool of colleagues treated her very well. In the press box "I always felt really welcome," she said. And her place as one of only a handful of women in those circumstances made her stand out. "They all knew me."

The special treatment extended to the multitude of players she used as sources too. It's true that some players were less apt to talk to her due to her gender, but this went both ways. "There were players who would talk to me more because I was a woman." During those years, her gender gave her opportunity to broach subjects that might have made her male counterparts feel uncomfortable, but not all. She acknowledged that plenty of male reporters are capable of asking sensitive questions. "I could ask players questions that would maybe make them feel vulnerable, and instead of not answering, they were more likely to open up to a woman than a man."

She followed this up with examples of questions about family relationships, their failures, and their flaws—types of questions that might make a player defensive. "I think women often can more easily project a sense of caring or at least goodwill," she explained.

But it wasn't always just game-day stories Joan was producing. Leading up to the Barcelona Summer Olympics in 1992, she became deeply involved with the sport of gymnastics after a conversation with her editor at the *San Francisco Examiner*, Glenn Schwarz. One day they started talking "about sports in which girls can be the best in the world, they can be the Joe Montana or Michael Jordan before they reach puberty."

It was a topic that wound up becoming near and dear to Joan. Joan's coverage began with the reporting of swimming, gymnastics, tennis, and figure skating. She later narrowed her focus to gymnastics and skating, because they had the most in common.

Joan's series of articles led her to write her first book, titled *Little Girls in Pretty Boxes: The Making and Breaking of Elite Gymnasts and Figure Skaters,* in 1995. The book followed the stories of young girls and women who are at the top of their sports, and the stresses and problems associated with competing at the elite level.

Joan was approached by an agent after her series of stories were published. The agent, Jenny MacDonald, convinced her to write a proposal—the first one of which she admitted was "bad." But MacDonald kept taking her out to lunch and explained that she should rewrite her proposal, and that's when Joan's "Catholic guilt" kicked in. As she explained her thought process, "Well, she's buying me lunch, so I better rework the proposal."

That refined proposal was ultimately purchased as a book to be published by Doubleday Dell Publishing Group Inc. of New York in 1995 and later published as a paperback with Warner Books Inc. of New York. It would be named to *Sports Illustrated*'s "Top 100 Sports Books of All Time" list in 2002.

Coming from a reporting background, she went into the writing process optimistically. "I thought I could write it in six months, because when you're a daily newspaper person, six months? I could write *War and Peace* in six months!" It ended up taking two years. Included in this was a single year sabbatical that she took from her day job. "I'm always amazed when people can churn out their books and still keep their day jobs. I couldn't."

The book features tales of the high price of elite gymnastics and figure skating, stories of extreme eating disorders and heartbreaking injuries, the type that don't just ruin competitive careers but that ruin lives. Stories like that of Julissa Gomez, a gymnast who passed away in August 1991, three years after becoming paralyzed while performing a difficult vault at a competition in Japan.

And that of Christy Henrich, a gymnast who had once been

a real contender to make the 1992 U.S. Olympic team, but who sadly passed away at age 22 of multiple organ failure due to half a decade's worth of severe anorexia; anorexia that had caused her weight to drop to less than 50 pounds before her death. Both Gomez and Henrich were coached by Al Fong.

At the time of its publishing, the information Joan revealed in the book caused quite a stir. Of it *Booklist* said, "It's a nightmare vision that may forever change one's image of those Herculean efforts by such Olympian pixies as Olga Korbut and Mary Lou Retton." The *Village Voice* concurred, saying "Read it, and you'll never watch either sport in quite the same way again."

Joan knew she had written something extremely powerful that resonated with a lot of people. She explained the impact the book had on the viewing public as, "now we can no longer close our eyes to the price." She clarifies she is not against girls participating in gymnastics altogether, but said that through her research for the book, she learned that "elite gymnastics is really not something that should be pursued."

In the end the book received a lot of praise, as well as a lot of criticism, for that matter. But in the beginning she felt pressure about writing the book because she did not know the sports of figure skating and gymnastics very well. "The reporting had to be impeccable," she recalled. "There couldn't be a single error in that book because the entire thing would have been dismissed."

The reaction within gymnastics itself was mixed. She was covering the 1996 Summer Olympics in Atlanta and attended an initial gymnastics press conference leading up to the start of competition. It was also attended by approximately 200 reporters and gymnasts crammed into the space, sitting elbow to elbow at the table on stage. She stood up to ask a question of coach Marta Karolyi and received funny looks. It was like a chain reaction as it dawned on them, "That's her! Oh, my god, that's her" is how she described it. "I was like the devil woman. And I really was to USA Gymnastics," she said of the sport's governing body.

Marta and Bela Karolyi have long been ingrained in USA Gymnastics, first as coaches and later as executives and administrators. Marta has held the position of national team coordinator since 2001.

But on the positive side there were individual gymnasts who told her, "That's my story. I'm glad somebody told my story." Her reputation with USA Gymnastics notwithstanding, *Little Girls in Pretty Boxes* did make an impact in the sport. "They put out a really comprehensive book for parents that I thought was really admirable," she said, referencing USA Gymnastics' Athletes Wellness Program.

She's quite proud of the outcome of the book, asking how often do you get to feel like "you actually have maybe made an impact on people's lives, somebody changed, somebody listened?"

The association's criticism was harsh, but it didn't totally turn Joan off from gymnastics. American gymnast Kerri Strug had one of the most iconic moments at those 1996 Atlanta Games and seamlessly landed her second vault on an already injured ankle to help her team, then dubbed "the Magnificent Seven," to win a gold medal. People assumed that "I would just jump on it," Joan said. Instead, in her writing about that night, she labeled Strug a "warrior." "I was proud of Kerri Strug for doing that. I absolutely thought that was the right thing to do," she said. "I think she made the decision every athlete was going to make."

Approximately four years after finishing *Little Girls in Pretty Boxes*, she wrote a book proposal that her agent called *Big Boys in a Big Box*. The proposed book would have addressed the lasting effects of concussions and other injuries on former NFL players. "They finished playing football, and then they were gone, and we just turned our eyes to the next big star," is how she referenced it.

At the time, various publishers told her no one would be interested in the book, so she still has the proposal of a book that would ironically be of great interest to people in 2016. The truth of the sport and its problems are similar to what happened after her exposé of elite gymnastics. "They've ripped the facade off of football, and you can't pretend that you don't know what goes on."

Since then Joan has written multiple books, including her recent release, *Molina: The Story of the Father Who Raised an Unlikely Baseball Dynasty*, about major league baseball player Bengie Molina and his brothers Jose and Yadier. She collaborated with Molina to write his and his siblings' story of growing up in Puerto Rico with their father and playing baseball. The siblings, all who play or who have played the position of catcher, won a total of five World Series.

She got to know Molina in her most recent role while he was playing for the San Francisco Giants. "When Bengie decided to write a book, he came to me first, and so we collaborated on it," she said.

She enjoyed the process of writing a book with Molina, but telling someone else's story came with its own challenges. She explained that as a writer you're at the mercy of your subject's time, and after collecting all of their information, you must roll up your sleeves and "figure out how to tell this story with all these different strands and narratives."

"I loved writing the book," she added. "But it's not as satisfying as something that's wholly your own."

In 2006 her son had a traumatic brain injury. Joan took nine months off daily reporting to care for him. At the time, she was working for the *San Francisco Chronicle* and writing long, take-out features and a column. The prospect of continuing to write her column had become too mundane. "In journalism if you start getting comfortable, you're not doing your best work."

Coupled with that was the fact that she was told if she gave up her column, she would have to do "a couple of weeks a year of nights reporting on fires in the Mission District," she said, referring to the neighborhood in San Francisco bordered on one side by the 101 Freeway. The night beat didn't appeal to her, so she took a buyout. "I felt like I didn't leave journalism, I felt like journalism left me," she said.

Being away from the newsroom for nearly a decade has made her heart grow fonder for the little things, including "the messiness of it, the bad coffee, the complaining." She genuinely misses "being around really smart, engaged, curious people," she said. Journalists are a rare breed, and people like them don't exist in the civilian world, she added.

As for what she doesn't miss: the fear that comes from having to churn out a reporting assignment and hoping that you got everything correct in the available time period. "I don't miss that angst of taking those feelings to bed with me most nights," she said. "Just hoping that you didn't do something to embarrass yourself." At the end of the day she doesn't regret moving on though, because it brought about positive change. "You have to make yourself uncomfortable or else you're not growing."

At the time that she left the *San Francisco Chronicle*, she had a contract to write a book about her experiences caring for her son after his accident, but she didn't want to be at home writing the book five days a week. Her solution was to take a lot of people out to lunch and say, "I have this skill set. How can I use this skill set to make money while I'm writing my book?"

One of her lunch companions was Larry Baer, President and CEO of the San Francisco Giants baseball team. She knew him from her work as a journalist, and he had been very helpful in setting her son up with the best neurosurgeon in San Francisco after his accident.

She pitched Baer on the fact that the team would be starting the 2008 season without controversial star Barry Bonds for the first time in more than 15 years. She was convinced that the team needed a good media person to represent it as it moved into a new era. The job that she was pitching herself for has become more common in recent years as media coverage of sports has ramped up. "Teams in general are more aware of how important media training is and getting guys on board to represent the organization well."

Since then she has been working for the Giants as a media consultant. Her duties include everything from writing blog posts for the team's website to pitching stories to the beat reporters who cover the team. It's something she understands well after more than 25 years working as a reporter. "They're actually appreciative to have a good story," she said.

She helps the two sides, reporters and players, understand each other too. "If a player is acting like a jerk to a particular reporter, I can go talk to the player." It usually involves explaining where the reporter is coming from and that it's nothing personal. "That's also been really satisfying. To be that go-between in a way that I really understand both sides now," she said.

One of her biggest duties is to train young players coming up from high school, college, and the minor leagues on how to deal with the intense media scrutiny that comes with playing professional baseball. To Joan it comes down to one guiding principle. She asks them, "What do you stand for as a man? What are your principles in life? If you know who you are and what you stand for, then every interview will be guided by that." She believes that dealing with the media is now an important part of their jobs, and the best way to go about it is to be prepared.

She explained her tactics in detail. "The first thing I ask a player is, when you retire from baseball, and your name comes up in conversation among Giants fans, what three words would you want them to use? Integrity, hard worker, good teammate, selfless, socially responsible—whatever it is," she said. "The next question: how will the fans know about these traits? They can't know simply by watching you play. They know you through the media. So approach interviews not as obligations but as opportunities to let people know who you are and what you stand for as a man and as an athlete."

Overall, according to Joan, being a good journalist comes down to two specific things. "The main one is curiosity. If you don't have genuine curiosity, it's not the business for you." The other, "You've got to really care about being accurate. Really care about facts."

Many times writers are told that to get better, the solution is to write, write, write, but she actually sees it as read, read, read. "Just feed great writing into your brain and it's more likely to come out."

For all the aspiring sports journalists out there, she recommends brushing up on your knowledge of "the sweet science." "I always said that if you can't write about boxing, you can't write." She believes it's because boxing is full of rich detail, and that detail is available for all of the journalists covering the match.

Just like the concussions that have plagued the NFL, as a journalist the head injuries associated with boxing can be a bitter pill to swallow. "You're repulsed by it and totally attracted to it too," Joan said.

As for how she feels about sports journalism in today's climate, she thinks it's possibly the best it's ever been. She has concerns, though, that today's sports reporters aren't able to "stretch out and write those really deep character profiles," due to a lack of room in the daily paper.

A lot is expected of sports reporters too, including live tweeting the games. She wishes they had the ability to sit and immerse themselves in the experience of the game again. On the other hand she appreciates that today's journalists aren't shying away from the big issues like domestic violence and that "there's way less protecting of your local franchise."

Photo credit: Doby Photography, NPR

Chapter 7

SONARI GLINTON

AFTER SIX YEARS IN FINANCE, Sonari Glinton was laid off from his company in 2001. He didn't know where to turn next, but he found help from an unlikely source: the employer who had let him go. The company provided former employees with assistance from an out-placing firm. Before long Sonari had polished his resume, and it was just a matter of identifying places where he was eligible to apply. He decided against returning to finance.

As part of his journey with the career search, he looked to a "dream board" he created. His personal mission statement: "To have a career that allows me to use creativity to further the understanding between different people."

Sure enough, that's what he finds himself doing every day in his job as a business desk correspondent at National Public Radio, or NPR, as it's better known. "That is why I became a journalist, because I could tell stories to help bring people together," Sonari said. "I know that sounds cheesy; that sounds disgusting, but that is actually why."

More specifically, Sonari was determined to connect those people through radio. That's why most mornings he starts his day at about 5:30 or 6:00 a.m., working from home. On holidays he allows himself a later start but he only pushes his start time to about 6:30 a.m.

He works from home for the first hour or two, sorting through emails and exploring what's trending on Twitter. He also tunes into the *Marketplace Morning Report* and checks out various news sites. Most of his morning is spent "reading into the day."

That was a discipline Sonari picked up during his time as a producer for *All Things Considered,* one of NPR's most popular newscasts. As a producer for the show, a job he held from 2007 to 2010, he had to "be able to look at the board and have an understanding of each of those stories," or the majority of them, anyway. "I should definitely have an understanding of the stories that are leading the hour," he explained.

Sonari also makes a point to diligently listen to NPR. "When you work in the industry, you can't have a conversation with your best friend if they've been on the radio that morning and you didn't hear it. You *can,* but it's much better to know what your friends and colleagues are doing."

Once he's "read into the day," Sonari lets it all soak in while he goes for a run to get amped up for the day ahead. Finally, he heads into the office in Culver City, California, a 20 minute-drive from his home in West Hollywood.

He's in the studio by 9:00 a.m. on a typical day, he said, which might sound like a pretty full schedule to fit in by the time most people are starting work. Even more ambitious is that he started even earlier than he let on.

"I read the newspaper before I go to bed because it comes out early-ish here (in California). By bedtime, there's a full *Washington Post, New York Times*. Usually, I read those at night. The most important part of my job is knowing, having an understanding of what is going on in the world generally."

On a May morning in 2015, Sonari described the day's storyboard as touching on "the White House's ISIS strategy. It's going to be a week in review. I know that. Camden Police and I know there's a Camden Yards story, because we're following up on (the) Baltimore (riots). There's a lot of profiling stuff, Cuba diplomacy, Eurovision is happening this weekend. I just want to know what we're putting out."

At the time, Sonari was just wrapping up a piece called "How an African-American Ad Man Changed the Face of Advertising," which aired on NPR on June 15, 2015. "It's a story about a character we're calling the Black Don Draper," referring to the lead character, played by Emmy winner Jon Hamm, in the AMC hit *Mad Men.*

Sonari's NPR piece, though, focused on a man named Tom Burrell, "and it looks at how advertising has changed to include minorities. There was an actual person, an individual who pushed that."

"Black people are not dark skinned white people …" the story dramatically begins. To complete that "featurey piece," which ran five minutes and 21 seconds long, Sonari worked for roughly a year. "There's always long range, really short range, and then there are these projects that are in between," he said.

For the advertising story, Sonari sat down with Burrell in Chicago to talk to him face to face. "We try to avoid the telephone because people tune out when they hear phone sound too much. We want to have someone live and present. That's a part of the extra layer."

The approach added personality for this particular story, at least, because listeners could hear the moments when Sonari and Burrell were laughing together on-air like old friends. During the piece, Burrell told the story of when he got his first big break in the 1960s. It involved a white executive at his company asking him to sing "down home songs" for the company Christmas party. Sonari and Burrell both gave a belly laugh at that point.

The story about Burrell's rise in the advertising industry also became somber at times, which was interesting for the listener to hear over the airwaves. At other points in the story, there were dramatic pauses, brief moments of silence, and Burrell's solemn tone of voice, which signaled to the audience that he wasn't always willing to have a sense of humor when it came to the conversation of race. Those moments are what made the story so powerful, and they would have been challenging to convey in print.

For instance, here's a short clip of the banter between Sonari and Tom Burrell:

GLINTON: Burrell worked his way up from the mailroom to ad writing. But in those days, ads were pretty generic—you know, one-size-fits-all—and not a lot of black people.

(SOUND BYTE OF ALKA-SELTZER ADVERTISEMENT)

UNIDENTIFIED CHILD: With Alka-Seltzer, (singing) relief is just a swallow away.

GLINTON: And when they did try to do ads focused at the black consumer, they often got them comically—sometimes insultingly—wrong.

Burrell remembers an ad for Schaefer Beer that hearkened back to the days before the Civil War.

BURRELL: The line was: 1856—that was a very good year for beer.

GLINTON: It was a very bad year for black people (laughter).

BURRELL: And this ad is showing up in *Ebony* magazine. And it just screamed insensitivity. It was a horrible year for us.

It wasn't enough for Sonari to interview Burrell and let him talk about how influential he was in transforming the industry to market to minorities directly. Sonari needed legitimate outside sources to opine on the drastic changes the advertising industry has seen since Burrell's time.

He chatted with Robert Klara of *Adweek*, who spoke to the need for marketing to diverse groups of people with specific messages. An even bigger get for Sonari, though, was sitting down with Keith Reinhard.

The name probably isn't familiar, but the famous jingle he wrote *is*: "You'll feel better knowing anytime, anywhere, like a good neighbor, State Farm is there."

"I got the guy who wrote the State Farm song to sing it to me," Sonari said, taking a pause to reflect on that moment himself.

It's not unusual for Sonari to be in awe of some of the opportunities he's had, having reported from the Sochi 2014 Winter Olympics and the White House, as just a couple of examples.

On a standard schedule, however, he could be working on anywhere between three to five news spots if it's a busy day. If it's slower he'll record one news spot at most. "As a rule, I do at least one news spot a day. I'm on the air at least once, five days a week," he said.

Recording a 40-second spot might sound pretty quick, but Sonari points out "you have to interview people for everything." Most news spots are reserved for breaking news, but Sonari has pre-recorded several news spots too.

For example Sonari wrote and recorded an obituary for Vegas singer Eydie Gorme of Steve and Eydie, the husband and wife singing duo. And he wrote it before she ever died.

It's a common practice that isn't often discussed but is critical for the news business to turn around quick stories about legends of an industry—whether it be in music, automotive, or technology.

If people didn't know it was a typical practice, they did after *People* magazine mistakenly posted an online obituary for iconic actor Kirk Douglas … while he was still alive. The accidental post appeared online in November 2014.

Despite the mishaps, it's a practice that NPR continues. The iconic Tony Bennett is another who was still alive at the time of this publishing, yet Sonari recorded his obit years ago, and it is one of his favorites.

"There are certain people who are icons and they're at a certain age," Sonari explained. "This is an American war hero who's also an incredible artist who helped invent American pop singing. You don't want to do that on the fly in a couple of hours. You want to give him the respect his career is due."

Oddly enough, writing and recording obituaries was something Sonari did a lot of during his early days in radio. "I did a lot of spots years ago because, when I was a producer, it was a way to get on the air to learn, and obituaries are low-hanging fruit. There's no deadline," he said, adding, "You can make good ones. It's a minor theme, like pop music is kind of my jam when someone like that passes away."

Doris Day is another, like Bennett, who is still alive, but Sonari recorded an obit for her about six years ago. "She's never going to die. That's not happening," joked Sonari about the 92-year-old *Pillow Talk* star. "She's not going anywhere. She's released an album and been on NPR twice since I did that."

But when that day does come, NPR will have something ready to go, more or less. It will need an intro with the date and cause of death.

"A lot of reporters start off as producers. The way it used to work is you would get paid extra for doing extra work. That's why I did a bunch of them. I got paid $40 six years ago, or whatever it was back then to do those spots, because I wasn't an on-air person."

If it has Sonari's byline on it, he did the writing, research, and on-air reporting. "I pull all the tape and tape quotes. If you hear me talking, not only did I write the words, but I decided that is where that should go. 'This is where the sound byte goes. This is where the sound goes.' I take that and write that down into a script. I record my voice tracks, give the audio to a producer for a show, and then they mix it together.

"They make sure I'm to time, that there are no glaring errors, that the sound is not too weird. They get it ready and put it on the air. Then hopefully, while they're doing that, I'm making a call for the next story."

When arranging his interviews, Sonari always has to consider how he can collect the best sound.

Back in January 2015 he interviewed former Hyundai CEO John Krafcik when he was the TrueCar president for a "goofy story about how currency fluctuations influence car interiors." He described it as a very "NPR-like story," because it aimed to explain some part of the economy that's slightly complex.

Rather than sit down with Krafcik at the company headquarters, Sonari had a better idea: conduct the interview from inside a car. "I'm often making people do a thing. 'Show me how this works, drive with me.' If you're doing another kind of story, you're not going to necessarily ask, 'Can I drive with you in your car and interview you?' That may not be necessary."

Sonari said in this case it provided motion and a relevant narrative for the piece. "It's not enough for me to tell you a wonderful story. I have to break up the sound and move it in a way that's not expected, to keep you listening, that engages you, that makes you think."

Sonari wrote a piece about golf courses during the drought in California that was so severe Governor Jerry Brown issued a state of emergency and mandated residents to ration their water supply.

"We often are talking about the things that aren't clearly business, to see how do we get a wedge into the story. I think that is a hallmark of the newer editors on the business desk at NPR. I think one of our goals is not to be like 'The Nightly Business Hour' or 'Today on Wall Street ...'"

So rather than talk about how the California drought affected residents, Sonari had another angle: water was hard to come by, and places like golf courses came under scrutiny, so he focused on the story with a business lens.

Logistically, "I went to the golf course and interviewed everyone. I made everyone come to the golf course that I needed to talk to for the story so I could be in one place."

It gets complicated asking people to make it work for radio, but it's necessary. "You can have all the information in the world.

You can fill a graph, do as many visuals, talk and write as beautifully as you want, but if you don't have a tape, you don't have a story."

So the process of setting up interviews might present more challenges than just picking up the phone to make a cold call and get a few comments, but radio correspondents can appreciate the end result.

Debbie Elliott is a national desk correspondent based in Mobile, Alabama, and she described radio as "very intimate, in some ways. When you don't have the pictures there that television provides, the challenge is for us to make pictures in people's minds with the radio we produce," she explained.

She's worked for NPR for more than 20 years and, like Sonari, knows the importance of gathering sounds and piecing those elements together to create a story. In recent years her job description has evolved in many ways as NPR's website has grown to incorporate more than just audio.

Debbie's a radio reporter at heart, but she—along with her fellow NPR reporters—is also being asked to write online stories for digital visitors, interact with her audience via social media, and even, in some cases, create video packages. "That's the changing world we live in," she said. "It's all coming together."

Debbie teamed up with Oxford American on a few occasions to produce enterprise stories using video for NPR's website. In 2014 she helped co-report "A Black Church's Dilemma: Preserve a Building, or Our Identity?" The five-minute-long piece centered on a historic church in Helena, Arkansas that encountered financial and racial issues while raising funds to restore the building.

Although she conducted interviews, Debbie's voice was never heard throughout the video—a rarity for a radio journalist.

A few years earlier she reported on a video, "Mississippi Losing the War With Obesity." The video was somewhat lengthier—running at almost 12 minutes—and zeroed in on the state with the nation's highest obesity rates. She interviewed health experts and several obese people willing to discuss complications associated with the Southern state's serious health problem.

"That kind of work is very rewarding. Those kind of pieces are the kind of pieces I think NPR does like nobody else does," Debbie said. "The ability to be able to work on stuff like that, and be able to bring those voices and issues to the forefront, is what I totally love about my job."

Technology has evolved not only across NPR's website but with the equipment the reporters use. When Sonari started in public radio a decade ago, "before flash cards," he said they would "record people on tape and FedEx the tape. We would have to wait that step. Now we have FTP (file transfer protocol) files," which sounds easier, but sometimes we're "waiting for them to upload and they get corrupted, and there's a whole level of anxiety and difficulty around gathering sound.

"Again, the difference between that and a newspaper: you could have written down that someone told you where Jimmy Hoffa's body was buried, but if you don't have it on tape, that's a disaster."

Sonari keeps a kit nearby at all times. In it he has multiple microphones, batteries, cords, and more. "This kind of cord goes to this machine. I'm hooking up a thing where I can get audio out of a television set. There might be a moment where the only places I'm going to be able to get sound is by plugging it up."

Sonari has two drawers filled with cords and equipment. He spends about an hour every other week organizing his bag, playing with the cords, and making sure he knows where each piece is.

Erring toward the side of obsessive-compulsive-disorder is okay for a good radio reporter, Sonari said. "I always think what if you're a radio reporter who's at the hospital in Dallas when John Kennedy gets there? You better have batteries. You better have enough tape, storage left on your sound card, and have the right microphone—always."

Another layer is that in some cases collecting audio serves an archiving purpose as well. "When I'm there at a primary, and you get that speech from a podium, that's not only for your story. That is a historical record."

Being prepared to capture sound was something Sonari learned as a rookie, he said. In his case that came later than other journalists.

In his first internship he recalled the first weeks where they "just send you out and record stuff. It's so basic. It's the first and most important thing you do. You always have to be doing it.

"I can overcome a mistake that I make. I cannot overcome not having batteries. I cannot overcome if I don't hit record for that interview," he explained. "In radio, we live, breathe, and die tape."

It might sound tedious to anyone else to practice with a record button, but Sonari's early days required a lot of patience. He interned and then went on to freelance. By the time NPR hired him full-time, Sonari had four years of experience.

"It took me several years to get to the point where I was a journalist. It was the opposite of overnight. It was years and years of waiting tables and all that stuff, a lot of dues paying."

He worked at places like Joe's Be-bop Café and Jazz Emporium on Navy Pier in Chicago. It was a stretch from his previous career in finance. For most of his mid-20s, until he got laid off, he'd been employed at a big company called Cargill. "I could have gotten another job immediately. I didn't have to get laid off, but I remember thinking I didn't want the job. I didn't want to be in finance."

Losing his job, Sonari said, "was so important. It makes you believe in God. It was so vital that that happened when it did."

The company offered Sonari and other former employees help to land a new job. He set the scene back to 2001 when, as he noted, computers weren't as ubiquitous. "They'd give you a computer and a place to work, a phone, and you could have some place to look for a job. They would also give you classes like 'how to do a resume.' "I went to every single one of those classes. Resume, how to talk about your job, how to get a job, how to think about it, and all those things."

Sonari vividly recalled the time he was asked to describe when he was the happiest. His first reaction was to tell how back in college he wrote a column for the school paper and hosted a radio show. "Every person in my group said, 'That's what you should do.' It wasn't like I didn't think I should, but it hadn't occurred to me. I didn't know any journalists. I didn't know it was a thing. I barely knew what public radio was. Public radio is not—to my ever-loving dismay—ubiquitous in the black community."

It wasn't until Sonari was approaching 30 that he found what he wanted to do. Before that, "I wasn't one of those career-minded, driven people," he said. "From 30 to 40, I went from intern to correspondent at NPR. That's a relatively short time.

"Pick a direction and walk it. Walk towards there, because even when you're walking towards that, you're going to be picking up skills that will help you when you decide to change directions. But it's the dithering that will harm you."

So he took a chance and applied at WBEZ, the NPR affiliate in Chicago. He had doubts about whether he could realistically make a living doing it. "A lot of young people have a lot of angst. They're like, 'Should I do journalism or blah blah?' Who has it ever hurt to have a career in journalism? Even if you decided to go to medical school, now you're a doctor who can talk. If you go to law school, now you're a lawyer who can write. There's no career in which journalism can't help you." But, he warned, it requires commitment and, oftentimes, sacrifice. That could take the form of financial sacrifices or having to make geographic changes.

In his first 10 years in radio, Sonari lived in Chicago, Boston, D.C., Detroit, and, now Los Angeles. "Let's take a friend of mine, Ari Shapiro. He's lived in Miami, D.C., London, a stint in some other towns. Tamara Keith lived in Ohio, San Francisco, Washington. If you want to be a national journalist staying in one city, I don't know how you're going to do that. If you can, good for you. You might be able to do it in New York or L.A., good luck with that. Even in Chicago it's getting hard to stay. I think that's common in journalism. If you want to move up, you have to move."

But journalists usually see big rewards as a result: "In one year I went to 26 states. I've interviewed CEOs of huge companies, been there for technological advances, after tornadoes, and crazy things." Being there: that's truly the greatest payment, he said. "Nobody's getting rich in public radio, but you can live a life, feed yourself, and stuff."

As hard as it is, Sonari said it's worth it to be a part of this evolving industry. Take NPR. It relies on contributions and sponsorships for its revenue model. Every news organization has been hit with financial struggles and the decision to rethink its revenue-generating strategies.

"I think there are going to be some survivors. We're going to learn the financial model to give us information. It's too important for us to have it be free. I believe the end of journalism isn't nigh, at least radio."

Sonari admitted that the disruption that hit newspapers five to 10 years ago took longer to trickle into radio and harm its business model. "People weren't going to sit down and listen to a radio story on the Internet. But as soon as that got created, and people go to the two white earbuds, that is an existential threat to radio. It's an existential threat to the way we do business. But it's also an opportunity. Everybody with an iPhone can be a listener."

That was proven when the *Serial* podcast took off in 2014. It was the fastest podcast to reach five million downloads, boasting more than 40 million downloads that year alone, according to CNN.

Sonari and his team recognized radio's potential from the *Serial* success that got audiences asking, "'What's this podcast thing?' Right now it's not exaggerating to say in public radio, this is the moment, this is it, whatever *it* is. I'm not sure what the moment is, but this is it. We feel it here … The shift is coming, the revolution is happening in radio."

For Sonari this movement might help public radio solidify itself on other fronts too. Compared to newspapers, Sonari said, "Public radio is very new. We have an inferiority complex. We feel bad that we're not *The New York Times*. People feel like 'the real journalists are over there. I'm just doing this radio thing.' That is not how I feel, but that is a common trait among public radio people. The great inferiority complex."

Any time, though, that Sonari compares himself to other types of journalists such as broadcast TV people, he quickly remembers: "It's kind of the perfect thing. You get to do real journalism, get to talk to people, you get to have fun, and be in all the places. And you get a bit of your personality to show on stage a bit. But fewer people know me than know the weatherman in Pocatello, Idaho. That's the best of all worlds. No one knows or cares who I am, but I occasionally can be the person who tells the country a thing. That's awesome. It's the perfect amount for my ego."

Photo credit: Dawn Bowery, LAWAC

Chapter 8

TERRY MCCARTHY

BACK IN THE 1980S, FOREIGN war correspondent Terry McCarthy used to own a shirt that read: "*No me tires, yo soy periodista!*" That translates in English to: "Don't shoot me. I'm a journalist."

"It was kind of a joke because there was no question in those days that anyone would shoot a journalist," he said. How times have changed. Seventy-one journalists were killed in 2015 alone, according to the Committee to Protect Journalists, and 46 percent of them were working in war zones.

Terry, who speaks six languages, has covered wars since he started as a freelance reporter in Central America in 1985. His journalism career spanned almost three decades until 2012, when he was appointed president and CEO of the Los Angeles World Affairs Council, which has hosted eight U.S. presidents and more than 250 foreign heads of state and government over the past 60 years in order to provide an open forum for cultural diversity.

He's worked across the U.S., Europe, Asia, and Latin America while with *TIME* magazine, ABC, and CBS, among other outlets earlier in his career. He's taken on politics, business, military, social and environmental issues, and more, but he is best known for his work as a foreign war correspondent. His work abroad earned him four Emmys and an Edward R. Murrow award in 2011.

Now that Terry has transitioned away from journalism, he's opened up more about his personal experiences. He isn't restricted any longer, as when he was a traditional reporter who "isn't allowed to speak in the first-person singular."

He wants everyone to know that "war is really, really bad."

"People die. Sometimes wars are unavoidable, some wars are justified. I don't think many people would dispute we should have fought Hitler in the Second World War, but it comes with a cost. And I think the fundamental reason for a war correspondent doing what he or she does is to remind people there is a human cost to whatever conflict we have and so you will think really hard the next time you declare war on anyone anywhere in the world," he said during a 2012 panel, "Reporting from the Danger Zone," hosted by the Los Angeles Press Club.

Terry most recently worked for CBS and regularly found himself being introduced on national television by Katie Couric on the network's *CBS Evening News.*

One of his most notable pieces came in 2010. He was embedded with the U.S. Marines in southern Afghanistan for four months. His series, "The Thundering Third," profiled a Marine battalion, some of whom were tasked with the dangerous job of scanning for and removing IEDs, or improvised explosive devices.

Terry and his cameraman initially started covering the Marines during training at Camp Pendleton near San Diego, and he eventually followed the men and women into battle. "We got to know them pretty well, and they came to trust us," Terry said. "They allowed us to join them on the front lines."

In that particular report for CBS, Terry covered the deaths of several soldiers. Others were wounded, including Sergeant Johnny Jones, who lost both his legs and suffered trauma to his face during an explosion.

Behind the scenes, Terry recalled Johnny's commander asking "How are you doing, son?" And Johnny's response was: "Sorry I screwed up, sir."

"He was a brave man," Terry said. The cost of going to war was precisely what Terry was determined to show to viewers back at home. He got some pushback, though, from New York-based producers because he said there is a long history of U.S. media outlets not wanting to show Americans injured or killed in combat. "This is very disturbing footage, as you can imagine ... The media does not like to show dead or dying Americans. You can show dead Iraqis or dead Taliban because they're somehow alien, but we don't show dead Americans. In fact for the longest time you couldn't even show the coffins of dead Americans."

In this instance he said senior producers thought showing Johnny's missing legs would be too gruesome for the evening news audience.

"I said I didn't really care what anyone else felt about whether we should have been there or not, that I felt it's absolutely crucial to bear in mind that whenever the United States considers going to war — wherever, whenever, for whatever reason — it is imperative to remember this will cause casualties both to us and to whomever we're going to be fighting ... This is not a decision that we should ever take lightly.

"I won that argument. CBS showed the footage," he said, adding that the piece received positive feedback from viewers.

The series was awarded the prestigious Edward R. Murrow award, named annually in honor of the late broadcast icon who himself covered World War Two live.

Terry's team also won a national Emmy award, his fourth win. "Doesn't actually matter all that much to me, but it is nice to honor all the people who collaborated in the work — cameramen, producers, editors, etc. — particularly since they were all done in war zones," he said.

During a speech he gave at the Ebell, a historic social and philanthropic venue based in Los Angeles, Terry shared statistics on the injuries and fatalities in Iraq and Afghanistan alone.

About 50,000 soldiers were wounded. Of them about 1,500 were amputees like Johnny, the marine included in his Emmy-winning story about The Thundering Third.

Even though many soldiers have since come home to the U.S., Terry makes it clear: "Their war is not over ... These guys' war will last for the rest of their lives. They'll need medical care. They'll need treatment. On top of the number of physically wounded, there's an unknown number of mentally scarred soldiers with post-traumatic stress disorder. And that's something I feel quite strongly about that we need to keep in mind."

Terry said, without "wanting to elevate the role of a foreign correspondent," post-traumatic stress disorder (PTSD) is a real struggle for many journalists. Of course it is widespread among our military, but he pointed out the vets at least have the U.S. Department of Veterans Affairs and other programs where they can turn to seek help. "I think that really hasn't been looked at enough. A lot of journalists do have some problems, and I do have friends who have problems. I think we've hidden them a lot," he shared.

Terry thinks there's a lot of truth to the cliché of a hard-drinking war correspondent and that the roots of the abuse of drugs or alcohol often lie in their reporting experience of what they saw in the combat zones. "You don't go into this to be a war junkie. But the flipside is that you become one ... Once you've done a few wars, your bosses think, 'Oh, he or she gets it.' So the next crisis, put her on a plane and fly her in ... So you accumulate over the years a bunch of wars, and yet you're meant to be indestructible. Because you're not being shot at. You're not a soldier, so it's okay. You can just check out of your hotel and fly to the next war.

"And I think a lot of journalists probably don't even know what they're struggling with, but you know, divorce rates are very high among foreign correspondents, on top of alcohol and drug abuse."

Attempting to keep a healthy work-life balance, even from abroad, was crucial for Terry's state of mind. When he was sent to Iraq, for instance, he said it was pretty easy to make calls home since there were satellite links. So he often made several calls home a day. But in Afghanistan he and his crew relied on phones that only worked outside. "By and large, even from the desert, I was able to call home pretty frequently, and that was very important."

Noting that the calls could cost several dollars per minute, he said, "That was a privilege that was paid for by the network.

"A lot of the troops may only be able to call home maybe once or twice a month because they don't get it free, and they are not able to pay a huge amount for satellite, but it is hard to be stuck out in the desert and try to get in touch with your family."

Phone calls home weren't the only solution. It was important he have time off to actually fly home to see his wife and children in person. "I think people deal with the stress differently. For me, every time I came home it was a very welcome and necessary period of decompression. We knew what was in Baghdad was totally abnormal and unreal, so you make out as best you can, but it's not an easy thing to do."

He always had to keep in the back of his mind that he could return home to his "alternate life" with family, so he'd remind himself, "There is a better life outside of this crazy situation."

Keeping a grasp on the positive wasn't always easy. Especially on days like May 17, 2007, when two of Terry's colleagues from ABC were killed. "That was very tough. These guys did nothing wrong, and they were just journalists who were killed on a list that is far from short."

The cameraman, Alaa Videen Aziz, and sound man, Saif Laith Yousuf, "got caught up in a sectarian slaughter that was going on in Baghdad" in 2007, Terry recalled. They had been stopped in a car that night on their way home.

Alaa was reportedly driving, and when he realized what was going on, he tried to run away but was shot first in the legs to stop him from running and then was executed by being shot in his head, according to Terry.

As for Saif, "they wanted to let him go initially because he was a Christian and this was sectarian-driven," Terry believed. "They said, 'We don't have any fight with you,' but he tried to argue with them and said, 'No, this is my friend. Leave the cameraman alone. The two of us will stick together. Let us leave. We don't mean you any harm' and so they shot him, I think before they shot [Alaa].

"That was very tough, and we had to go public with that. We chose to go public in a straight way, you know, talked about what happened, but it was not a good day."

Terry and his producer didn't have time to immediately grieve. They were back to work the next day. They had a spare camera with them, so they were expected to continue reporting while "keeping their mind on the job."

Terry said it was always crucial to keep safety in mind, whether he was reporting from Burma, Afghanistan, or Egypt.

Almost inevitably, Terry relied on a fixer, a must for a foreign war correspondent. The fixer has local contacts, sets up interviews, and helps reporters to understand the culture of the city and how to survive. "In general we cannot function without them," Terry said.

A fixer is typically someone in the home country of the war zone who wants "somebody to help them fix [a particular issue], and they know their own government isn't going to do it. Be it Bashar al-Assad or Al Qaeda or whomever it might be. And so they come very bravely to western news organizations to help us out.

"I have a huge respect for all of these local fixers whose names are never known. We all know Dith Pran from *The Killing Fields* movie, but there are thousands of Dith Prans out there whose names will never be known, but without them we could never get you the stories that you see," Terry said.

He continued by saying that his trust in fixers is tremendous. He's gone into multiple situations where, had a fixer not been present, "something very, very bad could have happened. They understand the local situation. They'll tell you when to get out and how, and if you don't listen to them, you're foolish."

Up until September 11, 2001, Terry said fixers were the main protectors for foreign war correspondents. Post 9/11, though, journalists, particularly those like Terry who were working in Baghdad, usually have to have private security guards.

In Baghdad "foreigners were being kidnapped, and journalists, too. They were well-trained special forces and had guns, and they were acting as bodyguards." It was specifically unsafe in Baghdad, "where there was a high kidnapping rate. They knew if they could kidnap foreign journalists, they could get a lot of money for it. Or on some occasions, you found journalists were killed quite brutally."

For Terry and his fellow reporters, it became more than an issue of security but a hit to their reporting as well. "Nobody could really report on Al Qaeda or the Taliban without the risk of being captured or killed. It wasn't a lack of enterprise or lack of courage. It was just physically impossible to go out and talk to the other side because they would kill you, or they would kidnap you." So all the correspondents could do was to report what the U.S. military said, what the local Iraqi government there said, and try to pick up any scrap of information from civilians on the streets.

Terry doesn't have many regrets in his career, but he was really disappointed with how western journalism was forced to change post-9/11. "I do regret that halfway through my career, 9/11 happened and changed reporting the way I had described—with no access to one side of the conflict. It made it a lot less rewarding. It made it a lot less gratifying because you knew that you would only be getting half the story. So I regret that, but there was nothing I or anyone else could have done to change it.

"9/11 became our story, our reaction to it in Afghanistan later on. Whatever you think about the rightness or the wrongness of the reaction, the fact is that is what the United States did, so we followed it around. It was a tough time, and a lot of people died, and reporting suffered because of the lack of access to both sides."

Right before Terry transitioned to broadcast journalism, he worked for *TIME* magazine, most recently as the bureau chief in Los Angeles. Even then it was difficult to report on both sides. For one piece in particular, he remembered sitting down to read one of his team's 10-page stories about the Iraqi conflict. He realized there was no Iraqi quote in the entire piece.

He said that "giving a voice, and a true voice, to people on the ground" is one of the foremost important tasks of a foreign war correspondent.

His transition from *TIME* to ABC was a relatively smooth one, he said. The logistics, of course, were different. "For TV you need all of this equipment. You need sunshine, camera, lights," he said. "For print reporting, all you need is a notebook and a pen, and you can get a story."

But the TV producers were mainly interested in his background in reporting from a combat zone, versus his Irish charm or public speaking skills in front of a camera.

One adjustment for Terry was broadcast's shorter deadlines than when he was with the magazine. When Terry was with *TIME*, he typically had at least a full week to work on a story. With broadcast, breaking news is constant and usually must be reported on at least a daily basis.

With CBS he experienced an unusual work-sharing situation when he covered the uprising in Tahrir Square that ultimately led to the fall of Egypt's president Hosni Mubarak. There were three correspondents, each with a producer and camera crew, sent to Cairo. They all stayed as a team at a hotel right there in Tahrir Square, the epicenter of the story where locals were protesting their leader and demanding he step down as president.

"When we arrived in the middle of the story, it didn't take much imagination to see what was going on with them; you just stared out your window. The stories were right there on your doorstep.

"You're following breaking news every day," regardless, Terry said. But since there were multiple reporters on site, the work was typically divided into one person focusing on the 7:00 a.m. news for New York, then someone for the afternoon, and the third journalist worked on digging up stories for the evening news.

"There were some difficulties getting around Cairo. A lot of the streets were blocked and so often it made it difficult."

One day Terry went out to the Great Pyramid of Giza to do a story on the evaporation of tourism. But while he focused on that feature, his colleagues had to stay on the ground in Tahrir Square to cover the main action. "At one point it got quite scary because the government tried to blame the uprising on foreign interference and call the press to the ground. They sent their guys on to the street with pretty brutal instructions to beat up any foreign journalists they could find. The primary identifying factor of those was a television camera, so there were a couple of days when it just became insanely dangerous to operate TV cameras."

Terry described how "a lot of cameras were broken and smashed, and a bunch of journalists were hurt, and pretty quickly we stopped sending people out with big cameras." Many journalists resorted to using flip phones and cell phones to shoot video because it was not identifiable that they were with the media.

Civilians were extremely worked up and shouting slogans in support of the revolution. And with those crowds came extreme chaos.

Terry's colleague at CBS, Lara Logan, became probably the most famous victim. She was allegedly assaulted and attacked by a mob of men. She shared details of her experience on her show, *60 Minutes*, in a 2011 interview with Scott Pelley.

Logan was on assignment when her fixer, Bahaa, who was Egyptian and spoke Arabic, informed her it was time to get out of there. He heard a man saying, "Let's take her pants off."

"Before I even know what's happening, I feel hands grabbing my breasts, grabbing my crotch, grabbing me from behind," Logan said during her *60 Minutes* interview where she recounted the events. "I mean, and it's not one person and then it stops, it's like one person and another person and another person."

Logan continued to describe the struggle, detailing how her clothes were shredded, and the mob of men pulled out wads of her hair; she told how she didn't think she was going to survive the attack.

It is unclear whether Logan was attacked because she was a reporter or if it was a random attack, but journalists are without question finding themselves in harm's way more and more. Deaths, imprisonment, and exile rates are all on the rise, according to figures from the Committee to Protect Journalists. As of February 2016, at least 1,182 journalists have been killed on the job since 1992.

"As the world is becoming more repressive, and freedom of expression is under threat, the threats that they face are growing," said Robert Mahoney, deputy executive director for the Committee to Protect Journalists. "We just can't keep up with it. In the past few years since 2011, the Arab Spring, there is a phenomenon of journalists who are increasingly becoming targets. The journalist has become the story."

Despite the dangers of being in the war zone, Terry knows that the role of a foreign war correspondent serves a purpose. Today Terry leads the Los Angeles World Affairs Council as its president and CEO. He isn't reporting, but his mission in many ways stays the same: to inform Americans about what is happening in the rest of the world.

As he told the crowd at the Ebell of Los Angeles in his 2013 speech on the foreign war correspondent's role, "When something important happens around the world, it's crucial that we have good information, not biased or information somehow spun … In the context of countries that have very strict press laws, very often it's the foreign media that gets the truth out [because] the local media cannot report it."

He added, "Our freedom in this country is very valuable, and it's deeply reliant on the free flow of information."

Photo credit: courtesy of Geoff Edgers (pictured, right)

Chapter 9

GEOFF EDGERS

As the old Kinks song goes, 'Hey, Mr. Reporter, how 'bout talking about yourself?' Geoff Edgers did just that in the 2010 documentary, *Do it Again,* which he independently produced.

The Boston-based newspaper reporter has spent his career working primarily in print, but in the past six years or so, he's dabbled in film and television. He's hosted two shows for cable TV and created two documentaries, one in partnership with *The Boston Globe* and the other on his own dime.

His independent venture in filmmaking came in 2010 as Geoff was dreading his 40th birthday. That's when he embarked on a fantastic mission to reunite the '60s rock band, The Kinks. The group hadn't played together as a full band in more than 40 years, but Geoff was determined that he could bring them back together.

The style of the documentary, which was directed by Robert Patton-Spruill, is nontraditional since Geoff himself appears in the film to help move along the action. He pontificates about the best rock bands of the era, shows off his wife and daughter, and invites the audience into his home. Especially shocking is that he surprises interviewees of the film with requests to play a Kinks song with each of them during their interviews.

The documentary is star-studded, but it also subtly tells the story of a newspaper guy trying to do his job and make a life for his family. In the offbeat *Do It Again,* Geoff inserts himself into the script in a way that makes it as much his story as it is The Kinks'.

In the film, he shares his honest gripes about working for *The Boston Globe*, his former employer of 12 years. He chats with his wife, Carlene Hempel, a journalism professor at Northeastern University, about budgeting for their mortgage payments while supporting themselves and their daughter, Lila (before their son Calvin was born).

Even though Geoff said he loved working for the *Globe*, financial concerns over budget cuts and layoffs were real worries for him and his colleagues. The movie might be primarily focused on the dream of a Kinks reunion, but any reporter can surely empathize with the very real financial struggles that come with a job in journalism.

At the time he created his documentary, *The Boston Globe* was undergoing drastic financial constraints—a precursor to three years later when The New York Times Co. would sell the media group to Red Sox owner John W. Henry for $70 million, a far cry from the $1.1 billion the New York media giant spent on the brand back in 1993. And Geoff wasn't afraid to tell what he really thought about the newspaper's cutbacks in the film.

"I'm gonna lose almost $20,000 a year. That's my pay cut," Geoff ranted during the film. "I told the ... fathead who runs the union—who's a moron—I told him that he should take the ... he's not gonna take the cut. And our dues are going to remain the same even with the pay cut. I told him I was sick of his Titanic of a negotiating strategy.

"The Times threatened all along that if we reject that proposal by them that they will immediately impose a 23 percent pay cut, so I get to keep my pension, which I'll never see in 2034, but I don't get to keep my salary."

It isn't so different than today with many legacy newspapers. Most recently, the *Globe* laid off two dozen members of its editorial staff and issued several buyouts in October 2015, citing "unfathomably difficult forces in the news industry."

The announcement came less than two months before the wide

release of the Sony film, *Spotlight,* which stars Rachel McAdams, Mark Ruffalo, and Michael Keaton. It tells the story of the *Globe's* Pulitzer-winning investigative team that took down the Catholic Church in 2002 after exposing a long history of sexual abuse among priests. The movie received rave reviews and won the Academy Award for Best Picture of the Year.

The *Globe* was also featured prominently in *Black Mass,* the 2015 film starring Johnny Depp as famous mobster James "Whitey" Bulger. It points to the *Globe* as the outlet that broke the news of Bulger being an informant to the FBI since 1975.

Reputation aside, the *Globe* is one of countless news organizations showing signs of struggle as it navigates this new wave of journalism in the digital age. Regional newspapers lost about 40 percent of their staffs between 2003 and 2012, according to Pew Research Center.

Geoff has since moved on to work for *The Washington Post,* which he joined in September 2014 as a national arts reporter.

The *Post* has undergone a lot of changes in recent years, particularly since Amazon founder and CEO Jeff Bezos bought the publication in October 2013, ending 80 years of local control by the Graham family.

No one has seen the decimation of the newspaper industry more clearly than the *Post's* union organizer, Fredrick Kunkle. He has been a reporter for the publication for 16 years and is one of the longtime staffers who has been heavily involved with the Washington-Baltimore Newspaper Guild. As the guild's news co-chair, he led the most recent movement to protect employees' pensions and healthcare benefits for part-time employees in a deal that was reached in June 2015.

The agreement also gave *Post* reporters access for the first time to their online metrics for the stories they write. The concession was noteworthy because metrics were increasingly becoming a part of performance reviews for reporters.

"Our future is online. There had been talk that [access to the *Post's* metrics] was proprietary, and they kept it close to their vests, but reporters want transparency," Freddy said.

He acknowledged it is a fine line of measuring the weight of story metrics, pointing out that an editor should have different expectations for online views coming from a reporter covering Hillary Clinton versus a reporter covering the local city council.

According to Freddy, there were many details of this agreement that were left open-ended and "vague," needing to be ironed out, but he and the union were pleased to at least have started the conversation. Some of the staffers in the guild were less impressed with how Bezos pushed back on other parts of the deal regarding slashes to benefits, pensions, and retirement benefits.

Geoff's take is a little different; he was part of a hiring spree that Bezos initiated with his takeover of the company. "I mean, I like the paper and Jeff Bezos. I probably wouldn't have been hired if he hadn't come in," Geoff said.

Geoff is in a unique position with his latest role. He works for the D.C.-based *Post*, but he telecommutes from his home in Boston. "I would never have even interviewed for the job if they had said I had to move down there, because my wife is a teacher. My children are here, my grandmother is 93 and here. We have chickens. I can't move," he explained.

He decided to renovate the bottom level of an old horse barn at his house and turned it into an office where he has his computer, official letterhead from the *Post*, his stereo, and even a little refrigerator.

On average he's gone about one day per week, sometimes even three days. "If I'm writing a story on an opera director in Detroit, I go to Detroit and watch him work," he said.

Then he visits the *Post's* D.C. office about once a month. "The *Post* was kind enough to give me a desk and a nameplate in the arts department," he said. "Everybody I work with, these brilliant people, Pulitzer Prize winners, are just incredibly welcoming and warm because they're thrilled to have help, more people on staff in the arts."

But largely, he works with his editors by phone and email. Because he covers the national arts beat, he's on the road more than with the *Globe*, where he was focused on the greater Boston area only.

Moving to the *Post* has brought new opportunities for Geoff. So far he's interviewed Tom Hanks, Jay Leno, and Kareem Abdul-Jabbar, and that was just in his first few months with the publication.

"The *Post* definitely opens the door. It's sort of what you do once you have the door cracked open," he said. "If you look at the *Post*, they're brilliant Internet headline writers. They know how to draw people in, but they also are very classy. That paper that comes out on Sunday has beautiful photography, lots of space for print. The stories I'm writing are long, and they're running them."

Geoff was grateful that the *Post* allowed him to write about Angela Lansbury, "who might not fit the demographic of 18 to 34, but is an incredible figure, really wonderful to talk to, and worth reading about."

Lansbury is a legendary film and Broadway star, best known for her role in the television program *Murder, She Wrote*. Given her age, it's daunting to think of a fresh angle that reporters haven't covered in previous articles. But that was the key to Geoff's take on the profile.

"One thing that's notable is she's 89 years old and a star. I called the Actors' Equity (Association) and asked them how many people are in Actors' Equity, and how many are that old," he said. The actors' stage union confirmed there was only one other person older than Lansbury in the association.

"She's the second oldest out of 50,000 people? That's a great fact, and suddenly you take this very brief interview experience, and this person who's been interviewed a million times, and you have a fresh angle on it, and a fresh thing you can spin."

Geoff's beat might appear pretty glamorous, but differentiating his story from every other entertainment news outlet is a running theme for his work.

Sometimes that's as easy as creating a quick blog with a handful of YouTube videos in it like when pop singer Sam Smith's popular anthem "Stay With Me" got slammed in early 2015 for copying the melody of Tom Petty's "Won't Back Down." The lawsuit was covered by just about every entertainment website in the world, it seemed. So when the news hit that Smith would have to pay royalties to Petty, it could have been a straight news story.

Instead Geoff opted to write a post that embedded five sets of popular songs from YouTube. The videos were songs of other famous artists who had been accused of being copycats, alongside the original songs that had allegedly been ripped off.

"Amy Argetsinger, who's one of my editors, when that Sam Smith thing happened, she sent out a note like, 'What do you think of this?' to me and maybe four or five other people. I happen to have one of those disturbingly detailed senses; I just know stuff that you shouldn't know. I said, 'Yeah, it's like that Ray Parker, Jr. thing with 'I Want a New Drug.' It's kind of like the Beach Boys.' I knew that stuff off the top of my head. I just punched it out. It took maybe two hours."

Other articles of Geoff's are just the opposite. They take a fair amount of time. Take his profile of Kareem Abdul-Jabbar. Geoff was with Kareem for two days straight.

"You hope you have a personality and common set of interests that can connect with them … Kareem loves jazz. I knew that going in. I like jazz too. He is a big reader. I'm a big reader. He's a Sherlock Holmes obsessive. I don't know much about Sherlock Holmes, so that's not what I bring up. But I see him on his iPod fiddling around, and I say, 'What are you listening to?' [He says,] 'I'm listening to this Cuban pianist …' You're having this conversation with somebody who you're not going to necessarily put in your article, but they're interested, you're interested, and you're establishing a rapport so that when you ask them a question like 'Why haven't you been able to get a coaching gig?' or 'Why do you think you're so misunderstood?' you're not coming across as a stranger asking a personal question."

The same for Jay Leno. Geoff wrote a piece on the iconic late show host's return to standup after *Saturday Night Live* comic Jimmy Fallon took over *The Tonight Show.*

One of Geoff's most star-studded pieces was that of Tom Hanks. He spoke to Steven Spielberg and Julia Roberts to round out the piece about Hanks, leading up to his Kennedy Center Honors Lifetime Achievement Award.

"I was able to get this story because of the *Post*, because of its size and reputation. That story might not have been available before to me," Geoff admitted.

After covering the Academy Awards and interviewing so many celebrities, Geoff has gotten used to it, for the most part. Tom Hanks proved to be a little different. Geoff sat down with the actor of *Big, Forrest Gump, You've Got Mail*, and *Cast Away* fame. Always thinking of digital opportunities, Geoff decided to surprise Tom at the end of the interview by playing a trivia game he'd made up in honor of Hanks' affinity for Apollo 13.

He brought in his videographer and recorded Hanks' responses to questions about the Apollo spaceships. (He got half of them right).

"It's nice to show a little dynamic. Then, you also never know when those are going to go viral. They might," Geoff said.

Video footage showed that by the end, Geoff was comfortable enough to joke around with Hanks—decidedly not star-struck. That's not his style; only if it's an interview with Sting will Geoff allow the child within him out to briefly obsess over a celebrity like he did during his documentary where he met and jammed with the former lead singer of The Police.

"If Sting told me that he would only allow me to interview him while I shined his shoes for two minutes, spit-shined, I would do it," Geoff said in *Do It Again.*

He was clearly joking, but still, that's coming from the guy who recently turned down an interview with Academy Award-winner Sandra Bullock. It's true. He planned to chat with her for the Tom Hanks piece, but when her rep would only allow for an interview via email, Geoff passed. "You just can't get information in an email," he said.

Rejecting Sandra Bullock really meant refusing to play the PR game, one he's familiar with. Reporting on arts and entertainment is just like any other beat, Geoff said. He knows the feeling of being played by publicists all too well.

He has been covering the Bill Cosby scandal, and one of his pieces addressed how theaters were dealing with the fact that Cosby was continuing to tour despite protests and customers demanding refunds. "It didn't make sense," he said. "All these people are complaining and returning their tickets. Why aren't theaters canceling or postponing? I knew there was an answer, but I just didn't know what it was."

"I called these theaters and they would say, 'I'm sorry. We cannot talk about this …' If they had Renée Fleming coming in to perform arias, they would be emailing me 16 times a week."

Accepting rejection is just part of the process, as Geoff proved in his documentary, *Do It Again*.

He had some great wins: jamming with Sting and *New Girl* actress Zooey Deschanel. But there were also many scenes in the film where Geoff made a phone call that went unreturned or opened a letter from a representative saying, "Sorry, said rock star is not interested in an interview with you."

This was especially frustrating when Kinks lead singer Ray Davies wasn't open to an interview. More than that, Geoff needed his permission to use the band's music in the documentary. Davies ultimately denied Geoff rights to the songs (or more accurately, never responded to the request), which limited how the film could be released. The rock-umentary aired back in 2010 on PBS in 20 cities. It was trimmed from its one-hour, 20-minute run time to a one-hour episode for the stations.

The film eventually led to a couple of TV shows for Geoff, but that's as far as the film went. With no rights to the music, Geoff was never permitted to release a DVD for sale.

Despite limited airplay, Geoff said, "It was an incredibly satisfying experience creatively. It was never a product I was going to get rich on."

The first TV gig Geoff got out of it was as the host for the Travel Channel's *Edge of America*. It aired for 10 episodes and took Geoff to some interesting events. During the show's run, he covered a fair in Stillwater, Oklahoma, where he sampled calf testicles, and in a separate episode, he watched a snake get chopped into pieces.

"As a journalist, Geoff Edgers is a curious storyteller," Travel Channel's former senior VP of programming and production, Andy Singer, told *The Boston Globe*. "He's also crazy and up for anything."

Producers at the American Heroes Channel also saw that curious personality in Geoff. They selected him to host *Secrets of the Arsenal*, a show that highlighted "fascinating and key objects that played important roles in our military history."

The most astonishing part is that he filmed everything during his "spare time." He continued to work full time at the *Globe* the entire time.

"There were times where I would leave to film the TV show Thursday night, film Friday, Saturday, Sunday out of town, take a redeye, and be back Monday morning at my desk," he said.

Geoff said his editor was supportive, but even still, "My primary job was to do a good job as a writer for *The Boston Globe* ... the management, they were not eager to help me work on this other career."

Even when Geoff's "second job" was something that would be produced for the *Globe*, he said the news outlet was hesitant to pour too many resources into it.

He co-directed a 22-minute documentary short about the Boston Marathon bombings called *5 Runners*. The story followed the five runners who were crossing the finish line at the time the first bomb went off.

Again Geoff chose not to hone in on the angle that most media would be covering, which was the bombing, with the three deaths and 264 injuries involved. Instead he focused his energies on taking a look at these five survivors on their journey to the 2014 Boston Marathon one year after the bombings. A *Globe* reporter had taken a photo of the runners finishing the race, and Geoff said he "wanted to know who those people were."

"I thought it was an interesting idea, and I was naturally attracted to it because I thought this is a different way into a story that's going to be covered by a lot of people," he said.

The short aired on BostonGlobe.com and resides there now.

The project ultimately cost the *Globe* about $35,000 between filming, travel, and other expenses. AT&T sponsored the documentary.

The news organization and AT&T paid for the project, but as a staff reporter Geoff does not personally see royalties from making the film. That's better than he made out on his independent documentary a few years earlier, though.

He dished out about $150,000 to make *Do It Again,* much of it coming from investors, family, Kickstarter backers, and about 20 percent coming from his own checkbook. "To have a film and have only lost $30,000, that's actually pretty good," he told *The Hollywood Reporter* in an interview in 2011.

Making documentaries isn't something Geoff necessarily will do again, but he's open to it. For now he's content with his position at *The Washington Post*. He's persistently followed national stories like the Bill Cosby rape charges scandal (and consistently been denied access to Cosby for an interview).

On the flip side, he occasionally gets recognized by big-time folks like Nancy Sinatra. "You are such a great writer @geoffedgers," she tweeted just days after Geoff's piece "Why Frank Sinatra Still Matters" ran online in May 2015.

"I've been at this a while. If you consider this is the greatest job I could ever have, it's taken until I was 44 years old of working hard to get that job," he said. "It's a dream job."

Photo credit: courtesy of Andrew LaVallee

Chapter 10

ANDREW LAVALLEE

As the deputy bureau chief for Greater New York for *The Wall Street Journal*, Andrew LaVallee has overseen coverage of a record snowstorm, a suicide outside of his office, and a political scandal at the state capitol. And that was just on his first day.

Since he took over his current position in January 2015, New York City hasn't had any shortage of news. He's been with the *Journal* since 2006. In that time he's worked as the senior arts editor, a technology and media reporter, as well as a special projects editor and life and style editor in Hong Kong. Needless to say he's juggled many jobs during his time with the company, so now he's used to taking on a chameleon-like role in the newsroom.

He shares the load with a second deputy bureau chief in New York, as well as the bureau chief for the region. As Andrew tells it, the three stack their schedules to make it work so that an editor is always available for the editorial team.

Andrew takes the early shift by waking up and tending to emails, starting at about 8:00 a.m. and arriving at the office by 9:00 or 9:30 a.m. on weekdays. There are other editors and an online editor who are already there, cranking out stories for the web.

But Andrew is helping to make decisions like "do we need to be sending people somewhere, and are there things on the schedule that we should make sure we have people attending?"

The New York bureau has about 15 reporters and eight to 10 editors. They are separate from the hundreds or more who work for the global headquarters from the same building but are looking for stories on a broader scale than the localized New York bureau.

Andrew directly oversees a handful of the team, mainly working with reporters on state politics, philanthropy, economic development, the New York suburbs, and Connecticut. His team works aggressively to put together the section that appears online everywhere but is delivered in print only to the tri-state area. They focus on local stories, but they are in close contact with the folks who put the front page together.

That is unless they rise to a level of national interest. Then the articles could appear in the national section, which is distributed to every subscriber in the country. "There's a national editor, and we'll sometimes pitch things to him, and say 'you might be interested in this' or sometimes he'll see what we're working on and say 'we'd like to see that,'" he said. "Page One kind of works the same way, like they'll keep an eye on things, and if they see a story they think rises to the level of Page One, then they'll let us know."

One recent example was when three men were arrested in Brooklyn and charged with conspiracy, because they attempted to board a flight to Syria to join the Islamic State, or ISIS. The story was reported by Pervaiz Shallwani, Rebecca Davis O'Brien, and Andrew Grossman and first ran online on February 25, 2015.

"It seems like every other day there's another American who's getting arrested on their way to get on a plane, but they were kind of the first, so that became a Page One story," he said.

"Our courts and crime reporters heard that these guys were getting arraigned. Then as we found out more, the story got bigger and bigger. Eventually, they said this is a Page One story. Let's get this together."

A story of that size requires a lot of information gathering and fact checking, but there is also the immediacy expected from readers. "You're really assembling the story piece by piece every couple of minutes. I really love that. It's a huge rush, but it is kind of an adjustment for more traditional journalists to think that way," he said.

In the case of the ISIS arrests, he said, "a lot of things had to happen at the same time. That's when you're really glad there are other people to work with, another deputy, another bureau chief, and other editors."

When the news broke, Andrew said they had two main elements to use: the men at the courthouse getting arraigned, and the complaint, which gave the details of the arrest when the charges came out. "We often have someone reviewing that quickly and kind of trying to glean as much information as they can about leads they can pursue."

The complaint was filled with information, Andrew said. Some people were digging up records, while others were searching to find where they might have family members and identifying any mosques where they might have worshipped, "just any places we could start sending people … looking for threads that they can pull together for the story."

"Back in the office where I and some of the other editors are—a lot of times you'll tap a reporter to be your relay guy, or the person everyone is kind of feeding material to. You're working really closely with that rewrite person to sort of figure out what needs to go into the story. Are there holes, things you need to be pursuing, or making calls on?

"That can be kind of a chaotic time because there's a lot of information pouring in, and you want to get a good, coherent story online. I guess one thing that's changed the last couple years is that it's not enough to just deliver that story at the end of the day. You want to get something to readers right away and keep updating it every time you get some new bit of information."

The urgency behind breaking news is a lot less lax than Andrew's old beat, which was arts and lifestyle. "With culture … there's breaking news, but it's knit differently by nature. It's not something where you're getting a piece of information, trying to build it out, and add to it throughout the day," he said.

The appetite for arts and lifestyle news is different, he said. Many people are looking at arts and culture coverage as a means to figuring out what to do with their spare time.

"You're keeping an eye on what's going on in the city, what you think readers might be interested in, doing lots of coverage you can plan out in advance. You're setting up photo shoots, and thinking about packages and video, and how do you have something really compelling and interesting for readers. As opposed to this thing just happened, how do we get information out there right away?"

Culture is more than a job for Andrew, he said. It's a beat that he could see himself exploring again someday. He's always had a passion for the arts and worked as Yoko Ono's assistant in his pre-journalism days.

He's covered several topics for *The Wall Street Journal*; his first was technology and media.

After deciding on a career change from working in technology and marketing for several years, he attended Columbia University School of Journalism. There he made a lot of connections, including people who worked at *The Wall Street Journal*. "They told me to go get some full-time newspaper experience and keep in touch. I did that," he said.

He took a six-month position with *The Patriot Ledger* in Quincy, Massachusetts. Then, as he was wrapping up the internship, he heard about an opening with the *Journal*. He applied, got the offer, and moved back to New York.

"It was a dream come true. I was sort of humbled and nervous about starting there. It was an incredible, lucky break. I treated it that way and took the work really seriously," he said.

Andrew started at "the bottom of the totem pole" as a junior level reporter. He was writing stories, but he just had to work a little more closely with his editors. "I was covering technology, but it's not like I was covering Intel or Apple. It was broader. My initial assignment was to write this story about what was going on with NASDAQ and the markets."

To accomplish that he had to be on the ground running at 9:30 each morning when the markets opened, and he would have a story up online by roughly 10:00 a.m.

"It was incredibly stressful when I started, but you get the hang of it. It teaches you how to be fast, and a story about tech stocks that runs in *The Wall Street Journal* gets a lot of readers, and people will tell you if you did something wrong right away. You learn to get the facts straight and be responsive to questions and tips that readers raise. Our email address is at the bottom of all our stories, so they know how to find you really quickly."

Two years into that first gig, he went to Asia for the first time on a family vacation. His mom is Chinese and grew up in Hawaii. His father is Caucasian of French-Canadian and Swedish descent and grew up in New England. Andrew still has some distant family in China whom he met during that visit.

"I had been curious about [Asia], and after I saw it I was more curious and really wanted to figure out a way to work there and get to know that part of the world. I had expressed interest when I got back and told people I was up for a change."

Soon after, Almar Latour, then managing editor of wsj.com, was promoted to run the Asian edition of the paper. "When I heard about that, I had a chat with him and told him I'd love to go with him and help him out over there," Andrew said. "He took me up on it."

Jumping from a position in New York to Hong Kong might sound drastic, or even surreal, but Almar said that the opportunity for *WSJ* reporters to move overseas for a period of time is commonly available. Many reporters "like switching up their experience" and working for the organization in various bureaus within the States or abroad. It's "one of the beauties" of working for the *Journal*.

"You can move to these faraway or even obscure places, and that can all be part of your career path," Almar said. "It's a huge cultural adjustment to go to another continent. That's part of the fun."

Almar was named publisher of Dow Jones Media Group in early 2016. But prior to that, he'd been promoted to executive editor for *The Wall Street Journal*. He said that in terms of hiring, the *Journal* has a universal quality it looks for in its staff: "People who are the best in their field in whatever stage of their career, people who have a real commitment to journalism, and people who are very dedicated to their craft."

When looking for journalists within the team who would be capable of being successful overseas, the *Journal* seeks out people who are self-starters and able to quickly set up a new network of sources. Andrew fit the bill, Almar said, because he was both "inventive and enterprising."

As Andrew described it, he wasn't exactly a foreign correspondent but "more of an editor" who was based in Asia. "It's not like I had to go there and learn a new language and figure out how to cover Chinese politics. There were other people who were doing those jobs."

Andrew's title was special projects editor, and he helped create and launch various digital products in Asia. There were a few country-specific blogs Andrew helped oversee, such as *Japan Real Time*, *India Real Time* and *Korea Real Time*, that capitalized on hyperlocal coverage.

"I would spend a week or two in those bureaus, talking to them about what sort of things we might cover and what they could be doing … It was really a digital job, teaching them how to think more digitally and do stuff in real time," he explained.

Then, the second year he was there, he was named the lifestyle and culture editor for Asia. "At that point I was more rooted in Hong Kong but working with staffers and freelancers all over the region. They were pitching me stories, and I was editing them and putting them together."

An example of a story that ran for *Scene Asia* was the rise of secret supper clubs in the region, published by reporter Lara Day.

It took some adjusting, but Andrew eventually became really

comfortable in Hong Kong on a professional and personal level. "There's a big, close-knit expat community, so when you move there, you make friends quickly because they've all been the new kid in town. They're very welcoming, which was a really wonderful thing. I also went there with my partner, so us being together also made it easier to get acclimated."

His partner, Marco Repola, fortunately had a job where he could work remotely much of the time, but as Andrew is quick to point out, Marco's not a journalist. "I'm often grateful he's not a journalist because it gives me a bit of distance from it. I have lots of friends who are in relationships with other journalists, and they're constantly talking about journalism and about co-workers and that kind of thing. We do plenty of that, but it is nice to have someone who disengages at some point. It's good for my sanity, I think, especially living overseas where your circle of friends becomes work friends-focused. He's friends with a lot of *The Wall Street Journal* at this point, and he knows all our usual griping and gossip and nonsense we talk about."

Connecting with people in the community was crucial for Andrew as he made decisions on what should be covered for readers.

Working for the *Journal* in Asia is tricky because even though the operations are much like an English-language newspaper, the audience is different than the American audience. "There's a lot of new wealth over there. There are a lot of people looking to the English-language publications 1) to help them learn English and 2) to help them learn more about how the rest of the world sees them … In China and Japan a lot of our readers are interested in how we write about China and Japan. It's a different perspective than they get from reading their local media."

But then of course not all stories written about Asia are exclusive to an Asian audience. "You've still got this huge American audience that wants to know about the whole world, so you do have to figure out how to make the coverage accessible to both.

When we were writing something, and it was running online and getting read in Asia during Asia daytime hours, not all of those stories ran in the U.S. paper," he said. "Sometimes they decided this isn't really relevant to American readers. That didn't stop us from doing it. We still thought there was value."

Even though Andrew's job was largely aimed at an English-speaking audience, the *Journal* is consistently coming up with ways to become more global. There are local language operations in China and Japan. "Mostly what they are doing is translating some of our English-language coverage. Sometimes it's just a matter of telling them 'I think this might be of interest to you guys.'"

"Increasingly they're actually writing their own stuff. Especially our Chinese language site, it's become a huge thing and developed into a life of its own. They have some native language speakers. One of them really knows Chinese real estate, so he writes a column in Chinese that has this whole following over there.

"There's another woman who is a super smart financial person and native Chinese, so a lot of times she's writing a column in English and Chinese. She does both things herself. She doesn't really need a translator. We are doing more of that stuff, which is really interesting and exciting to be a part of. If you don't speak Chinese, there's only so much you can do to get involved."

Almost three years later Andrew refers to his time living overseas as an "incredible learning, life-changing experience."

Another experience it gave him was how to serve as a leader and flexible worker, no matter which hat he happens to be wearing that day. "I really love writing. I think it's a fabulous thing in general. But I think that at least for now editing really suits me, and I like the collaborative aspects of editing. When I was a reporter, I often felt like I was doing my own thing. Whereas an editor, I feel, is more integrated into how the whole newsroom works because you're working with lots of different reporters. You're also working with people who are doing visuals and multimedia and with other editors. I really like that."

And Andrew really does work with people of all backgrounds. The reporters he works with do, *after all,* work for one of the most prestigious newspapers in the country, so they generally have a high level of talent. But Andrew explained that strong reporters still require guidance. "There are some reporters who are really independent and know their subject matter inside and out," he said.

Some of them don't demand a lot of Andrew's time, while others just want a different level of communication. "There are some reporters who really benefit from having a sounding board and someone to talk through ideas with," he said. "There are some people who more want to keep you apprised of what they're pursuing, like they have a narrative or threads they want to connect, and they know what they need for that."

If Andrew agrees with the reporter's angle, he'll "let them run with it," but that isn't always the case. "Sometimes you say no to things or have a different idea or shape a kind of story differently. It varies depending on the reporters and their relationship. I like that. I like having different ways of operating with different people. It makes it interesting and challenging."

Then there are constant conversations about whether a particular piece needs to "explain their corner of the world to a big pocket of people" or if it should be more narrowly focused for insiders in their field.

"Editors sometimes will challenge either of those approaches and say 'let's explain this to a broader audience' or 'let's talk about this interesting little thing because it's a good insider story.' I guess that's where an editor plays an important role. We're trying to tell all kinds of different stories and they just require different approaches," he said.

Editors at the *Journal* are also heavily relied on for fact-checking purposes. And beyond that, the newspaper is prepared to prevent and combat charges of incorrect information.

The publication has a standards group in place that aims to prevent errors from happening, like the erroneous article about a gang rape that allegedly occurred on the University of Virginia campus that appeared in *Rolling Stone* magazine in 2014.

"Virtually every story goes through more than one editor," Andrew said. The assigning editors direct reporters on their different stories. Then the story will go through the desk editor, who might be laying out the page for Greater New York or Page One. The online editor will also have a go with the story and get it ready for the web.

"Those people are also experienced, and they may see things I don't see," he said. "Having two people look at things helps. We think it helps make the work higher quality."

And if the story is sensitive in nature, the standards group will review the piece, along with the *Journal*'s lawyers in some cases. The standards editors and legal team also act if there is any legal action that arises as the result of a story.

"When you have something you think is sensitive, you get them involved before it runs so that they can help identify any red flags and make sure we've done our due diligence on the reporting end of things," Andrew said. "Having it go through them gives you this greater assurance that you've got a bulletproof story."

Photo credit: Greg Kessler

Chapter 11

S. MITRA KALITA

S. MITRA KALITA MADE A splash in early 2015 when she landed the second highest editorial post with the *Los Angeles Times*. As an Indian-American female journalist, her opinion has been highly sought after in journalism circles—whether it be lending her views for an op-ed about the future of digital journalism or offering her thoughts on minorities in the workplace during a speaking engagement.

Prior to her position with the *Times*, she'd worked for prestigious outlets like *The Wall Street Journal*, *Quartz*, *Newsday*, and the *Associated Press*.

It's been a long journey to accept that her leadership style might be different from a lot of other people—and that's okay. She has no problem admitting that there are people out there who write better and know more than she does.

"Nobody talks about this, but the older you get the more insecure you actually get in your writing and your journalism," she admitted. "When I was younger I would write columns and be very definitive and contrarian and go out on a limb ... Life gets more complicated. Stories get more complicated ... I actually hesitate to wade in."

This happened to her when she worked at *Quartz* and was covering the 2014 Indian election for prime minister. The issues surrounding the election impacted her on a personal level, but she feared speaking out because of what she referred to as the "brilliance" that was being published elsewhere on the *Quartz* site. In her role then, she commissioned economists, politicians, and other political experts to write about the future of the world's largest democracy.

Mitra believes taking the time she needed to write the piece helped her in the long run. "It forced me to take a very measured, personal, only from Mitra could this piece come out, column," is how she described it after the fact.

She has a graduate degree from the Columbia School of Journalism, but it wasn't in a textbook that she picked up all of her journalism credentials. As trite as it might sound, she actually learned a crucial lesson from watching the 1991 film *Boyz n the Hood*, starring Ice Cube and Cuba Gooding, Jr.

The pivotal scene that resonated with Mitra was when the character Doughboy's brother is killed, but it doesn't make the news. "Either they don't know, don't show, or don't care about what's goin' on in the hood," Doughboy said.

Mitra pointed to this scene as an eye-opener for media covering minorities during her keynote at the 2015 annual camp for the Journalism and Women Symposium. Being a minority is a thread that has followed Mitra throughout her career, and it's actually what spurred her into the news business.

She attended the Hugh N. Boyd Journalism Diversity Workshop at age 16 at the prompting of one of her high school teachers. She spent two weeks at the workshop in 1993 and, like most of her dozen and a half teenage colleagues, soon realized that journalism was the career path for her.

Mitra described the impact of the workshop mixed with the then culture of the '90s. The workshop's organizers tried to make them feel like they were needed in newsrooms, and their stories and voices were very much welcome. She admitted that it worked.

She attended college at Rutgers University in New Brunswick, New Jersey. While there she worked on the school newspaper, *The Daily Targum*.

Mitra said that she arrived on campus during "probably one of the biggest years of racial protests on campus since the Civil Rights Movement." The protests were due to an incident involving then president of the university, Francis L. Lawrence. In November 1994 Lawrence commented during a speech to his peers that underprivileged students do not score well on standardized tests because they do not have the same "genetic hereditary background" as other students. Despite the controversy and on-campus protests, Lawrence remained in his position as president until 2002.

By her senior year of college, Mitra ascended to the coveted position of student editor-in-chief of *The Daily Targum*. The controversy on campus had allowed her to recruit a diverse staff for the paper, their reasoning being that they wanted "the paper to be their own," she said, and to represent their viewpoints and various cultures.

Mitra was proud of the paper's presence during this trying time and said that for the first time it "enabled me to see the role of newspapers in a society," which is something that she would gain more experience with in the years to come.

She knows the importance of the minority voice but cautions that it isn't the only thing that matters when you get to the top echelons of journalism. "When they talk about the top job, they need somebody who's basically going to steer the ship, maybe save the ship," she said, speaking from personal experience. "You know the color of your skin really pales in comparison to your competence."

With that said, Mitra described herself as someone who is on some level "obsessed" with diversity in the newsroom, but she believes that diversity's greatest strength is the varied lenses that individuals with different backgrounds bring to their stories.

She has held numerous positions in journalism and has soaked in knowledge from every single one. At her first professional job in the industry, it was the tricky balance of writing both fast and accurately. The job was at the *Associated Press* in New Jersey in 1998, and it was a very memorable one. "I would be out in the field, and I would literally be dumping my notes, and because you're doing that over and over and over again, you become able to report out a situation and essentially craft what you're going to say in the moment."

She mentioned that this is an invaluable skill to have, regardless if you're a reporter or an editor. Working at the *AP* was a great reporting boot camp for the self-described timid 22-year-old who was initially afraid to pitch stories. Mitra attempted to work on this fear by attending the Columbia University Graduate School of Journalism in New York City, where she studied narrative writing.

After Columbia she made a stop at *Newsday* and covered diverse subjects, including the borough of Queens and immigration. From there it was a stint at *The Washington Post*, writing about schools and globalization.

Two important things happened to her in D.C. She gave birth to her first daughter, and she released her first book in 2003, titled *Suburban Sahibs: Three Immigrant Families and Their Passage from India to America*. The book follows the immigration experience of three families from their home country of India to the suburban neighborhoods of New Jersey.

John S. Major's December 2003 review of the book in *The New York Times* was full of praise for Mitra's writing style. "Modest in scope, but as shapely as fiction and as timely as this morning's newspaper, this book is an informative one to read for pleasure," he wrote.

India was Mitra's next career stop. She had heard through the grapevine that a man she knew and was working with at *The Wall Street Journal* was moving to India to start a newspaper. Her reaction was to send him an offhand email saying, "I'm so jealous!" He immediately contacted her and offered a job, even though he had yet to confirm her salary or exact title.

That man's name is Raju Narisetti, and he is the founder and former editor-in-chief of *Mint*. "I was looking for an early core of people that brought strong contemporary journalism standards, ethics, a sense of can-do, a willingness to stretch their own capabilities and learning, and an appreciation, if not understanding, of India, to help me create a one-of-a-kind journalism offering in India," he said with regard to his recruiting tactics.

Raju added that he believed Mitra, whom he hadn't worked directly with up to this point, could make a difference at *Mint* and he wasn't wrong.

Raju was pleased that Mitra brought something unique to the table at *Mint*, which today is India's second largest newspaper focused on business. He said as an editor that she is "curious, opinionated, but open-minded" and that she has "a desire to always make journalism and journalists (around her) better for audiences."

He added in an email that she is "impatient with status quo, personally and professionally. She understands our business is no longer just about longevity but is increasingly about relevance. And she knows how to straddle those worlds."

Mitra took a leap of faith by joining Raju in India for the launch of *Mint*. Working in India taught her how useful competitiveness can be in this industry, explaining that she received nine English-language newspapers on her doorstep every morning while living there.

She saw the work environment as, "everyone does journalism in fear of being scooped." That is important because "in a lot of newspaper towns that became one-newspaper towns, that urgency ceased to exist."

Her position at *Mint* was national editor, and she oversaw reporters covering topics like education, nonprofits, art, and those who wrote features. She also wrote a weekly column that was general in scope but often touched on what she refers to as "a changing India," the workplace, and gender.

Mitra wrote her second book based on this experience and titled it *My Two Indias: A Journey to the Ends of Opportunity*. In fact this opportunity allowed her to find some closure and answer a question that had followed her throughout her life: "What would have happened if my parents never left?" as she stated in a 2010 interview with Indian business program New Delhi Television (NDTV) Profit.

Initially, Mitra took a leave of absence from *The Washington Post,* but she never returned to her old job. In fact it was *The Wall Street Journal* that brought her back to the U.S., where she eventually became a Page One writer, thus enabling her to have a second child.

Prior to that she had been the senior deputy editor for the Greater New York section but had suffered a miscarriage. Doctors feared conceiving again would be difficult for her. Mitra felt she couldn't in good conscience continue in her editor role.

She credits "a fleet of editors who rallied around me" that enabled her to transition to a more flexible position where she was mainly responsible for herself instead of a group of 25 reporters. She is extremely grateful for their support to this day.

After her second daughter's birth in November 2011, she got a call from *Quartz,* the global business news division of *The Atlantic,* specifically produced for reading on devices. The team at *Quartz* offered her the position of commentary editor, and even though she wasn't fully ready to return to work, "the idea of going digital first appealed to me," she said.

So she went to work and soon became fully focused on the "Ideas Section." "We set about both reflecting the conversation on the Internet, as well as stoking a lot of it." That was her job for the next three years.

She continued to work at *Quartz* and was named a Spencer Fellow at Columbia University, which allowed her to research a book on school segregation. That book is still in the works, and Mitra described its structure as being about present day issues, the current state of school choice, and it asks questions about how children are currently being organized.

Writing a book is never easy, according to Mitra, but she said as an author you begin to get more and more involved in the topic. She described it as finding "subjects where you feel like you are the only one who can do it. And it sort of becomes like a purpose in the world."

She stays balanced by keeping up a schedule of writing books and working a daily job in journalism. She thinks she couldn't do one without the other and be truly happy.

After two years on the job, Mitra eventually became an executive editor at *Quartz* and even helped them launch the organization's India-focused page. Then in 2015 the *Los Angeles Times* came calling, asking for help on the company's digital strategy. Initially, she was resistant to leave New York, but she told the caller, the paper's editor and publisher Davan Maharaj, "Let's have a conversation."

That conversation progressed, especially because Mitra said she is "invested in local journalism working" and had interest in the paper's success. Plus, Davan gave her the hard sell. "I think he made a joke about it being 75 degrees and sunny and that the Thai food was better, and I kind of fell for it," she commented with a laugh. She joined the *Times* in May 2015 as managing editor for editorial strategy.

All of her reporting experiences have impacted her editing style. She refers to herself as a "fairly chaotic leader," mainly due to how much she has going on in her brain at a single time. Mitra sees a place in the newsroom for editors like herself and for those who are more "methodical."

She admitted it's morbid, but she evaluates her day-to-day impact in the newsroom by wondering what would go on if she were dead. "What would have happened if [I] never existed?" she sometimes asks herself. "What would be the stories that didn't get done, the thoughts and ideas that wouldn't have gone viral?"

Her strengths as an editor are in her ability to see the world anew each morning. She elaborated by saying, "I think a lot of reporters see it as wallpaper, and I kind of have been taught to look at a black, blank canvas."

As for what a reporter needs to do to get Mitra's attention, she's simply looking to be engaged and drawn in as both an editor and a reader. She's also highly ambitious for herself and those who work for her. "I have a lot of stories that I want to do," she said, adding, "I have a lot of stories that I want [other] people to do."

She wants stories done creatively and for them to be strong too. "I think a lot of people want to build their brand without having the substance," she said, making it clear that a writer cannot get ahead without substance.

After nearly two decades in journalism, Mitra has empathy for reporters working in the 21st century because so much more is being asked of them. "They need our help in both mentoring and decision making," she said.

She singles out that journalists' participation in social media like Twitter, Instagram, and Facebook is a job requirement at many publications now. Mitra believes that it plays an important role in the dissemination of a story. "There's a fairly fundamental organizing that social media helps journalists do," she said.

As an editor she has a special affinity for headlines and the ability they have to draw readers in. The kicker also holds extreme interest for her. "I think that the last thought of a story is so important. It either spins it forward or it leaves you with a feeling," she said. She's of the opinion that not enough people dwell on this.

When it comes to differentiating between newsrooms based on size, or even those that focus on print versus digital, Mitra acknowledged that there are fewer differences than most people probably assume. She did point out one main difference: print newsrooms are usually laid out in groupings that mirror the sections and the order in which readers go through the paper.

Despite a career in which she has moved around a lot, Mitra has very few regrets. She's been exposed to many different newsrooms. "I actually see that as a good thing," she said. She's observed that there are some similarities that she calls the "bedrock of all newsrooms," including the type of people who are attracted to journalism and an overall commitment to honesty and integrity.

She's also proud of the people she put in place at *Quartz* and appreciates how much they rallied once she left, calling it "a testament to that organization," and noting that their web traffic has remained strong in her absence. "I've been involved with startups for the last 10 years, and you never want to build something where you're crucial to the organization."

Like many journalists who were working back in 2001, covering the catastrophic events of September 11 was life changing, especially for those located in New York. Mitra was working for *Newsday* at the time. Already an experienced journalist at that point, she was forced to make some tough decisions while covering the aftermath of the terrorist attacks.

That specific morning she was in Queens at the dentist, but she kept fidgeting as she tried to watch the TV coverage of the attacks. Her dentist eventually shooed her out. Cell phones weren't functioning at that point, so she found a payphone and called into the *Newsday* newsroom.

Editors told her to "go to Manhattan and just walk." She estimates that her walk from Queens to Manhattan was about five miles, and on her way to the Queensboro Bridge, she took notice of a handful of Bangladeshi butchers shutting down their shops for the day.

The men were talking about their fear of Muslim backlash and how it would probably be similar to what they and their businesses faced after the World Trade Center bombing eight years earlier on February 26, 1993.

"And so without even calling the desk, I just made a decision then and there to cover the story," she explained. She interviewed the men and called the notes into *Newsday;* she commended the paper for going ahead with a special edition featuring the Muslim reaction.

"There are also all of their neighbors who suffered losses as well. They're dealing with a double sense of loss, right?" she said. "One of victimization and one of racism."

Next she made what she calls probably "the smartest move of [her] journalism career." She found an Algerian taxi cab driver and offered him $150 to drive her around for the day. She was grateful for the driver's presence that day because it provided an extra layer of security and allowed her to approach some of the diverse groups for on-the-record comments.

One of these articles, titled "Muslims Fear Fellow New Yorkers' Revenge," was posted at 8:00 p.m. on September 11, 2001. Mitra shared a byline with fellow staff writer Carol Eisenberg for this piece.

She called in additional interviews to the newsroom and worked with the religion reporter on the final story. "I like to think we had that before other outlets because of my lens on the story," she said.

Fourteen years later Mitra's role as a visionary has put her very much in demand. In 2015 alone she publicly spoke at the Online News Association's Conference & Awards Banquet in Los Angeles, the 25th Annual Asian American Journalists Association National Convention in San Francisco, and was the keynote speaker at the Journalism and Women Symposium (JAWS) Conference and Mentoring Project in Whitefish, Montana.

JAWS' former president Linda Kramer Jenning said the organization chose Mitra because they were specifically looking for a "woman newsroom leader" to inspire attendees.

The speech was titled "The Women Feminism Left Behind," and Mitra's husband, artist Nitin Mukul, and two children watched the speech from the front row—her youngest daughter even tried to join her on stage at one point. This is something that Jenning referred to as "the perfect picture of juggling work and life."

While she spoke, Mitra revealed that she often blends work and life. "I do work a lot. I also live a lot," she said. Although she said she doesn't require the same combination from her staff, it works in her sphere.

She's also extremely fortunate. Mitra was asked the inevitable question, "How do you do it?" by a follower on Twitter as part of her interactive speech. She answered in a direct and honest way, "*I* don't. *We* do." She referenced help from family members, neighbors, friends, and a nanny. The fact that her husband has never complained about her working too much or too late elicited a cheer from the JAWS audience.

"It's important that people see I have a life with my family; that has a lot to do with my journalism and how I cover our great city," she shared.

Photo credit: *The Seattle Times*

Chapter 12

MICHAEL J. BERENS

WHEN MICHAEL J. BERENS GOT the call from a reader saying "Your article saved my wife's life," he knew there could be no greater victory. And that's saying a lot, considering the national recognition that came his way in 2012 for the esteemed Pulitzer Prize he shared with fellow reporter Ken Armstrong for their investigative reporting when they were with *The Seattle Times*.

That phone call to Mike about a local Boeing engineer's wife was far from an isolated incident. Mike said he and Ken received well over a thousand phone calls, letters, and emails from locals wanting to express their gratitude for the series, "Methadone and the Politics of Pain," which was published as a three-part investigative series in December 2011.

Prior to the reporters' collaborative effort, methadone was the drug of choice in the state of Washington for patients seeking a cheap painkiller. As *The Seattle Times* investigation revealed, this seemingly cost-effective pill came at a high price for the state: It had taken 2,173 Washingtonians' lives since 2003.

But because readers took the time to read the articles in late 2011, many Washington residents' lives were potentially saved. And, to Mike's surprise, once-stubborn legislators took action by releasing an advisory to all of the state's physicians about the drug and removed it from the top billing as a first-choice pain prescription; it is now a last resort pill.

"This was incredibly gratifying. You put in all of this work, and you're actually making a difference in people's lives," Mike said. "That's the very nature of what a newspaper is supposed to be doing."

Starting with an unsolicited email tip from a Washington healthcare professional, Mike read the message and considered if it could be true that state officials were downplaying the effect this drug had on their constituents. But it didn't matter so much what Mike *thought*; it mattered more what his initial findings on methadone turned out to be.

Before he ever pitched the idea to his editors, Mike began by deciphering the email tip, which was full of medical jargon. Then, during what he refers to as his "hunting stage," Mike furiously sent out public records requests, scoured through information, and created databases of his own in order to prove the tip either credible or false. And when he broke down the note, he discovered relatively quickly that this investigation could be well worth the work.

Mike realized, "Okay, he claims that the patients are unnecessarily dying from methadone. Well, how many people died from methadone overdoses accidentally? So when I took the death certificate database, I hunted around, and I saw, 'Wow, there are thousands of people who have died accidentally from methadone overdoses.' Then the question becomes, 'Okay, how many of those people were taking methadone for pain?'

"It turned out about 98 percent of them were taking it for pain. Now I realized this [email] was partially true. So now is the state luring people to methadone as a way to save money?"

From there Mike read through transcripts from state committees and health administrators who chose which drugs to recommend for people on Medicare and Medicaid. "I saw transcripts with discussions where people *were* warning them that methadone had unique risks, and they kept ignoring those pieces of testimony," he said. "So I realized there is some truth to this; there *are* people who believe that the state is ignoring warnings in an effort to save money."

With that, Mike presented his case in a proposal to *The Seattle Times* after he discovered that all of the points on his enterprise project checklist checked out. His criteria included finding answers to:

- Is it new?
- Is there potential for change or reform?
- Can the issue be quantified?
- Will readers care?
- Are there on-the-record victims to bring the story to life?
- Why this story, why now?
- Is there a unique source of information?
- Can I describe the story in six words or less?
- Do *I* care?

Once he was able to satisfy all of his own personal inquiries, his methadone piece gained approval and he dove right into the extensive research stages.

Like most of his past investigative stories, he estimated the finished product was roughly one year away from completion. Mike continued to aggregate even more public data he found within records from the state's healthcare and government agencies. And since he was already able to connect the drastic number of deaths to methadone prescriptions for pain, he searched for faces to put together with the thousands of victims' names.

He stumbled upon the riveting account of a young woman whose testimony oozed of everything front-page news stories were made of: *"Two sisters critically injured in a car crash. Only one survives to tell about it; she had insurance and was prescribed oxycodone for the pain. The other, who had no insurance and was given methadone, dies."*

The surviving sister was willing to talk, so Mike was ecstatic for the potential impact from the parable he envisioned for his lede. Upon closer investigation, however, the story had some holes. As it turned out, alcohol played into the vehicle accident, the family had a history of felony convictions, and the surviving sister grew less committed to telling her story on the record. Ultimately, she wound up backing out.

Mike didn't pressure her to change her mind and go public. Rather he included her segment only briefly in his article without giving away all of the specifics about her. "I understood," he said. "It comes down to the honesty in why you are doing this. I said to her, 'Thanks for sharing your story with me.' It was powerful enough even to do one paragraph. So every interview is different. The secret is to just be really honest with people about what you are doing, why you are doing it, why you want to help them, and what they can get from the process as well."

Losing one interview didn't, by any means, point to a dead end. Mike knew he had to find new sources to fill out the greater anecdotal picture he wanted to portray to his readers. That's when he found Sara Taylor, whose daughter Angeline Burrell had senselessly overdosed on methadone.

Through a few introductory phone calls, Taylor shared vital information with Mike about her daughter's history with methadone — and critical to his story, medical records that he could only obtain through a victim or family member. Hidden in plain sight, the medical notes revealed that Burrell's doctor warned her that the drug could result in death. Sure enough, two days later that tragic prophecy was fulfilled.

As grateful as Mike was to have Taylor as a key source on this story, he explained, "It's not like Angeline Burrell was the only methadone victim out there in the state of Washington. There were thousands. This is just one person we had identified correctly, and then her mother was willing to go with the story."

He said it was important Taylor understood from the beginning that, by participating in this article, she had the power to save lives. On the other hand this article would live in the online world forever; it's not something that can go away if and when she wanted it to. So Taylor considered, and she proceeded to speak with Mike in four separate phone conversations and several email exchanges before meeting in person.

Anyone who saw the front-page story of *The Seattle Times* could instantly tell this had been an emotional interview. The lead photo shows Taylor sitting at her dining room table over a photo album open to her daughter's picture, while an unbearable flood of tears pours out, and her husband sits in the next chair, also pained with grief.

One of the reasons Taylor was open to a candid interview at her home with Mike is because, he said, "I don't come in like a salesman. I'm not selling anything. I'm in her home because she wants me there, and I'm really an observer."

Mike is just as capable of pulling information from those who are less willing to talk than, say, an interviewee like Sara Taylor. In the methadone story, for example, there were health boards and state regulators to pin down. Albeit a more difficult type of person to crack, Mike always maintains his policy of complete honesty up front.

The difficulty there is often exacerbated when he discloses he's an investigative reporter. "They know we're not running a feature story," Mike deadpanned. "I don't dance around what I'm doing; I have a really successful strategy that's worked well for me. I don't have to provide the specific avenues of pursuit [with every source he interviews] ... There *are* people on these stories who will camouflage what their real mission is. I don't."

As for those people in high places who are skeptical of participating in an interview with Mike, he tells them straight up, "It's not like I need you to tell us what's going on. I want you to help make it accurate and balanced. That's the pitch I make when someone perceives themselves as not being able to benefit from a story."

After going solo for six months on the methadone project, it sank in just what he had gotten himself into. "At that point I realized that there's a lot to do here," he recalled. "These stories are very technical, and you really have to be careful with every word, every description, and every fact quoted. And it takes a real amount of work to get this thing condensed down to be fair and accurate."

So Mike approached his colleague Ken before proposing the idea to his editors, just to feel out if he had an interest. Fortunately, he did. "We worked really well with each other," Mike said of the collaborative duo. "We can trust each other. I don't have to worry about whether he is going to get the right documents ... Both of us have different specialties that, when combined, create a really incredible team."

Mike's expertise comes in computer-assisted reporting, as well as building and analyzing databases. "If there is a secret ingredient to my stories, it has almost always been that the story revolves around a self-made database. I can go through death certificates and tell you the exact number of people who died in Washington this year.

"I know how to pluck out the people who died of methadone or how many died with benzodiazepine in their bodies. There is a database of in-patient hospitalizations throughout the state: I know how to read those medical codes and figure out who went in for heart surgery but had to have their sternum cut out because there was an infection inside," he said.

Ken's strong suit, Mike said, is the conceptualization of the story. "It's amazing how he is able to synthesize information down to really strong words, and he's just a terrific writer."

So while the preparation on the front-end was divided into separate specialties, Mike and Ken each contributed to the writing of the actual articles. "We weren't sure how we wanted to write the first-day piece. So Ken wrote a version and I wrote a version. With that we figured out what kind of voice we wanted with the piece, what kind of approach. Ken's first version I didn't care for a whole lot, and he didn't care for *my* version a whole lot, so we went back and tried it again."

From there Mike and Ken each alternated writing sections of the three-part piece and stitching it together. In the end Mike pieced most of Day Two together, while Ken wrote most of Day One. "His version versus mine for the top was much better. There is no pride in who does what. It's all about the process and not the ego."

Ken, who now works for The Marshall Project, a nonprofit criminal justice news site, has worked alone on several investigations and with a partner or team in other situations. "I find working with a partner to be more rewarding," he said. "You have someone to share your discoveries with, to bounce your ideas off, to correct you when you start going off the path. There are so many advantages to working with someone, particularly when the people enjoy working with each other. That was certainly the case with Mike."

He said that Mike is meticulous with data, and it shows in his reporting. "A lot of spreadsheets are dull and straightforward. Mike has all these layers," he said. "He prioritizes the data by a number system, he uses a color system to put in another layer of organization. All the yellow fields mean this, all the blue fields mean that. It sounds like too much. When it comes time to write and figure out what goes where, it's such a lifesaver."

Their partnership in telling a story worked so well that Mike actually partnered with Ken on another investigative piece two years later. The project centered on the biotechnology pursuit of cancer drugs and the profiteering of companies trying to make the next big money-making treatment.

"It's an anatomy of how the small biotech companies are competing with each other, trying to discover the next billion dollar cancer drug, and then all the shortcuts and illegalities and people that are hurt hard as a result of this race," as Mike described it.

The story, "Pharma's Windfall," ran in two stages in November 2013, both in print and online. And the team continuously brainstormed about how the data and images should be presented, both on the printed page and the website.

Mike knows that just the story, especially with today's technology and resources, isn't enough for readers' appetites. So he keeps up communication with staff photographers and graphic designers to make his stories visually appealing. That includes photos and videos for online versions of his stories, as well as graphics like the map in the online version of "Methadone" that displayed markers for each death in the area caused by an overdose of the drug.

"There are so many new tools out there to use," Mike said. "I'm always looking for tools that will help me do my job better."

And it's those very types of resources that Mike strives to share with his colleagues. He proved that when he and Ken donated their $10,000 Pulitzer Prize winnings back to *The Seattle Times* so more reporters could receive training by the Investigative Reporters and Editors (IRE), an organization in which Mike and Ken place a great deal of faith.

"My greatest hope is that one of our staffers will be sitting in a training session, and that proverbial light bulb goes off, and the next important story is born," Mike told *Columbia Journalism Review* reporter Olivia Smith in an interview about the donation to his peers. "So much public information is now maintained exclusively in a digital format. Yet, so many reporters don't know how to access and analyze it. Training is the key to unlocking stories."

Prestige now automatically accompanies Mike's name since he won the Pulitzer, an honor he was a finalist for twice before. But as meaningful as the award is to him, he doesn't allow it to define his work. "I know so many journalists out there who have done incredible work," Mike said. "On any given day there is work much better than mine, based on the fact that they got incredible results. And some of them have never received *any* award, much less a Pulitzer."

At a ripe 34 years old, Mike's work at *The Columbus Dispatch* scored him a spot on the 1995 Pulitzer Prize's list of finalists for his contributions in beat reporting. His story about the municipal justice system's discriminatory practices gained national attention after he had been with the paper for about 11 years.

He started out as a copy boy with the *Dispatch* and then worked his way up to the police beat. It was there that Mike really learned what the newsroom was all about. Even then Mike was grooming himself to be a solid enterprise reporter. But at a daily newspaper, each staff writer is expected to file stories every day, even if they have more in-depth stories brewing on the back burner.

"My editor's idea of an enterprise story was one that took *two* hours to write instead of one," Mike joked, with more than a hint of truth behind his words.

Yes, those beginning days at *The Columbus Dispatch* were eye opening for reasons other than just the pressures of strict deadlines. One of his first big scoops was with that newspaper, where Mike found himself facing the barrel of a .38 caliber handgun.

The reporters on the police beat had been hearing rumors of a major police investigation, and the alleged murder suspect was a William D. Wickline, Jr. "William was already in jail on another charge, and they were looking for the connection of a whole bunch of murders where someone had chopped up the bodies and then disposed of the body parts."

So Mike chummed up with local investigators and snagged the name and address of Wickline's girlfriend at the time. He took that information and went for it. The woman's house was along the route Mike took every night at about 10:30 or 11:00 p.m. on his way home from work. So after about three weeks of failed attempts from knocking on her door, she finally answered for Mike, and she was, of all things, pointing a gun at him.

Mike immediately suspected she was high on drugs. So he was more concerned she would *accidentally* pull the trigger, rather than shoot him down maliciously. "She made me take most of my clothes off. I had to take off my shirt, my sweater. She took my wallet to check my ID. She looked at my library card, my driver's license; I had an ID from the newspaper. She eventually put the gun down on the coffee table between us, and she started talking once she realized I was a reporter," Mike said.

"I wasn't scared. I mean, the only thing that scared me was my own stupidity. Even when she was holding a gun on me at the door, it wasn't like she was screaming at me, 'I'm going to kill you. I'm going to kill you.' It was her trying to decide whether she could trust me or not. Once she determined I wasn't sent to kill her then she started to relax."

And once that gun was down, Mike shared, "She talked very calmly about all these victims and how they stored their body parts in garbage bags and how the dogs ate it through the night. She went into great detail about it."

The next morning Mike was back in the newsroom by 5:00 a.m. to share his encounter with a more senior reporter who helped him create a "first-hand account" of the incident on Mike's behalf. "It was one of the biggest scoops I ever had. This was a huge crime story, and we were the first to break it.

"I was so exhilarated that I was going to break this story that I ignored the danger." To be sure, the unnamed woman in the article that ran on Page One was one of three women who alleged Wickline forced them to participate. It was expected that the women would receive immunity in the case.

But Mike learned two lessons in that one day: "Never go to a home alone, and always tell an editor if you are going to do something stupid like go out to the house of the girlfriend of a man who's accused of murder."

It was in those same early days, too, that he began honing his skills, even outside of work hours. He joined IRE, and when he attended his first conference about investigative reporting, he knew he'd never consider another profession. "As a young journalist, going to my first IRE conference was like seeing God," Mike said with a faint laugh. He was astounded to find, "There are thousands of people just like *me*, and they want to do better work ... I got to talk to people like Eric Nalder, who was a two-time Pulitzer-winning investigative reporter. He didn't know me, but I was able to sit down in a bar and talk to him and hear him talk. He was so cool.

"That really drove me, and I saw there is a higher purpose here. Here are a whole bunch of people who have the same higher purpose, despite whatever the small-minded editor or colleague I worked alongside wanted to do."

Mike built up his network through more conferences and also with the national recognition he already had achieved as a finalist for the Pulitzer. The *Chicago Tribune* was one such paper to acknowledge his accomplishments, and he went on to work there, initially for about seven years, investigating healthcare. Little did he know at the time he would return to work there in 2015.

"Going to the *Chicago Tribune* was very seductive because I got to travel the world and the country," he said. "I'd get national projects, so I'd go coast to coast visiting hospitals. It's intoxicating, it's hard and it's challenging."

On the other hand he was up against some heavy-hitting national news outlets to break those stories. "In the back gate I am looking over my shoulder at *The Wall Street Journal*, *The New York Times*, the *L.A. Times* to make sure they are not on the same track I'm on," Mike shared regarding the pressure from the harsh competition.

While working for *The Seattle Times*, he reported on captivating stories that invoked action from regulators and lawmaking agencies—like his IRE-recognized piece in 2012, "Glamour Beasts," about how "zoos' efforts to preserve and propagate elephants have largely failed," as well as his investigation in 2010 about adult family homes, "Seniors for Sale," that made him a winner of the acclaimed Worth Bingham Prize for Investigative Journalism and a finalist for the Barlett and Steele awards. Mike shared his second Pulitzer nomination in 2006 with Julia Sommerfeld and Carol Ostrom for their investigation "License to Harm." The piece investigated sexual misconduct by healthcare professionals and resulted in the tightening of state regulation.

He spent more than 10 years as an investigative reporter with *The Seattle Times*, and then he decided to give the *Chicago Tribune* another shot. "It doesn't matter what paper I work at, as long as I get to do the work that I think is important," he said.

And yes, after more than 30 years as a reporter, Mike still finds his work to be meaningful and exhilarating. "I can't imagine doing anything else," he gushed. "You read so many interviews of journalists out there, and they'll talk about that moment when they were first exposed to a newsroom environment and how you feel that magic and that electricity. And it's true. When you've been exposed to a newsroom and you go into any other kind of workplace, you realize it's just not the same.

"It's that combination of feeling like you're doing something important but having this incredible amount of freedom and heart; that's the elixir of the newsroom. I couldn't imagine finding a more exciting professional workplace.

"The newspapers have undergone and are undergoing a significant change, not always for the better. So it's tough to stay focused on what the real purpose of what we're doing is. That's how I maintain my enthusiasm, knowing that 'yeah, this is important.' What we do is *not* just a job. There are other people who are dependent upon the kind of job that you do."

Acknowledgments

From Stephanie:
Thank you to all my family, friends and colleagues who gave me support and encouragement throughout this incredible process. Thanks to Mitchel Storey, Toula Bianchi, Christy Bianchi, Craig Forshee, Chris Forshee, Andrea & Eric Nyberg, Chloe, Braden, Eliott, Tabitha, Connie Forshee, Chanell Copeland, Gregory Arroyo, Sharyn Obsatz, Thi Dao, the late Deenise "NiNi" Bianchi, and so many others. And thank you, Rosie, for joining me on this messy and beautiful journey.

From Rosie:
To all of the important people in my life, thank you. I wouldn't be here, putting the final touches on my first book, without your love, support, and inspiration.

From Stephanie & Rosie:
Thank you to Ken Armstrong, Nan & Biff Barnes, Tamara Bentzur, Alfredo Carbajal, Larry Dominico, Debbie Elliott, Meghann Farnsworth, Robert Greene, Fredrick Kunkle, Ryan Lambert, Almar Latour, Eric Lesser, Melissa Ludtke, Robert Mahoney, Jenny Margotta, Raju Narisetti for helping bring this book to life by acting as editors, sources, designers or by helping us create a solid Kickstarter project.

And, of course, thank you to the incredibly talented reporters and editors who gave us their time so we could share their amazing stories and inspire a new generation of journalists: Gilbert Bailon, Christina Bellantoni, Michael J. Berens, Geoff Edgers, Sonari Glinton, S. Mitra Kalita, Andrew LaVallee, Mara Leveritt, Carrie Lozano, Terry McCarthy, Joan Ryan, and Kendall Taggart.

Special Thanks to Our Kickstarter Backers Who Made This Book Possible:

Francisco Aguilera • Nathan Ahle • Pamela April • Gregory Arroyo • Sera Babakus • Brittany Barton • Liza Beres • Christy Bianchi • Travis Block • E. Frank Bluestein • Alison Boone • Bailey Brewer • Erin Burton • Dominic A. Cesario • Chhunny Chhean • Lisa Clark • Melinda Clarke • Ashley Cole • Frank Coletta • Chanell Copeland • Pat & Myles Corcoran • Tim Crowley • Richard Cruz • Thi Dao • Mary Delaware • Michelle DeRossi • John Dimatos • Carolyn Downey • Ethan Downey • James Downey • Victoria Downey • Linda Drucker • Maximilian Eberl & Julia Peitl • Rachel Ehrenberg • Muhammed El-Hasan • Robin Evenden • Arthur Faygenholtz • Grant Feek • Max T. Ferrikorn • Kevin Field • Susan Fishman • Pamela Flores • Julie Forbes • Craig Forshee • Judy Forshee • Aprille Franks • Sunny Freeman • Henry Fuhrmann • Mary Anne Gabay • Gabe Gazzola • Tom & Susan Haid • Amy Rosa Harrington • Sarah Harris • Amy Hercher • Rachel Hoffmeyer • Erin Horton • Roberta House-Forshee • Michael Hudson • Casey Hynes • Amanda Jones • Karen E. Klein • Deniz Koray • Tulin Koray • Brittany Krake • Beth Landry • James Leman • Rachel Lerman • Chris Lin • Cang Ling Yee • Marilyn Lucier • Melissa Ludtke • Lindsay Martin • Nellie Mazur • Brian Medley • Brian & Karyn Mehus • Athena Mekis • Tania Millen • Michael Morgan • Leah Motz • Becky Muldoon • Lydia Mulvany • Jo Mulwee • Carol Murphy • Waqas Naeem • Andrea & Eric Nyberg • Joy & Rich Nyberg • Sharyn Obsatz • Michael O'Connell • Marisa Paoli LeVeque • Erica Peterson • Jim Radogna • Dennis Raefield • Susanna Ray • Philip Reed • Richard Robledo • Isabelle

Rosenlund • Michal Rosenn • Becky Sarazy • Katia Savchuk • Courtney Shove • Joshua Singer • Leo Smith • Paula Smith • David Sprague • Kacie Stempel • Lynn Stock • Jerry & Theresa Stolaroff • Jesikah Stolaroff • Joshuah Stolaroff • Shaunah Stolaroff • Yancey Strickler • Brittany-Marie Swanson • Chintan Talati • Stephanie Tanner • Bernie & Carmen Tarkon • David Tarkon • Vince Taroc • Ashley Trevathan • Joanne Tucker • James Turnbull • Erica Veksler • Tanya Vidhyarkorn • Amber & Christopher Vincenz • Veronica Capron Vorva • Kelly Wadlinger • Joan Walsh • Kirie Taylor Walz • Samantha Westmoreland • Melissa Williams • Catherine Willbrand • Chen Yao • Beau Yarbrough • Tieg Zaharia • Annie Zak

CPSIA information can be obtained
at www.ICGtesting.com
Printed in the USA
FSOW04n2357190416
19290FS